**HU$H Money**

**The Sequel**

**#Stellaroseallday**

## Acknowledgements

Thank you to my soul tribe who went out of their way to make me feel special. Thank you for supporting my work, and for keeping me in a state of grace.

Thank you for loving me unconditionally and making me feel beautiful even when I did not feel that way.

Thank you for all the encouragement to keep going and for the gentile nudges in the right direction. Each copy of my memoir that people purchased I expressed gratitude to the universe, and I hope each one of you felt the good vibes. All the interviews, all the shout outs, and all the podcasts that brought me my sequel.

Many thank you's to all of you who made this possible, because no man is an island. I am incredibly grateful for every soul who supported me along the way. Even the critics gave me ambition and motivation to do better, when they called me a "Hot Mess" I took it but immediately corrected them and replied it's "Haute Mess." Then once again, I twirled on down my path into another rabbit hole.



ISBN-9798230003342

Cover design by: Art Painter

Library of Congress Control Number: 2018675309

Printed in the United States of America

# Epigraph

And when it is your turn, become SAVAGE. Tell them to be strong like you had to be.

Author Unknown

# Dedication

I am dedicating this book to me. I would like to thank me for showing up for myself when nobody else was standing by my side. For putting in all the demanding work, persevering, and keeping my nose to the grindstone. For waking up every day and rising to the occasion. For doing what nobody else was going to do for me. For staying focused. For continuing even when I felt like quitting. For believing in myself. For moving forward when I knew that more than likely I was writing my own obituary. My reward was learning that I am enough. That I have, and I do influence, and it started when I began to completely believe in myself, to stand my ground, and speak up even when I was not sure I was going to be heard by anyone but myself.

# Foreword

The aftermath of it all - the fallout. People ask me all the time if I recommend being a whistleblower and I say, "No", "Nope", "Not at all." And it's true, I do not recommend it at any time, ever.

It's like what they tell you when you're watching a dangerous stunt being performed, "DO NOT TRY THIS ON YOUR OWN. THIS STUNT IS BEING PERFORMED BY PROFESSIONALS."

There needs to be a large red warning sign posted somewhere about being a whistleblower. No, it has not been glamorous at all. This is something that you might want to think about if you're considering it. But if you do go through with it, how you prepare for it is going to make all the difference to you psychologically.

You see, before I decided to blow the whistle on them, they wanted to push me into a dark place and if they could not kill me, they were hoping I'd kill myself, and they tried everything they could to get me to that point of no return. Their plans where very well thought out and tactical. When I second-guessed myself, I had anxiety about it, and then I had depression about it.

Once you take a stand, it is not a situation you can buy your way out of. The psychological trauma is going to take a toll on you, and this is something of upmost importance. Yes, it will take its toll, and you will receive little support, if you receive any at all. Nobody will get why you're doing what you're doing, and nobody will be there to help you pick up the pieces either. But in the end (and most importantly), I got through the whistleblowing process by trusting the process and by doing it clean, without any type of substance abuse.

This was like walking a tight rope. Many would have handled what I went through very differently and succumbed to any number of demons, but in the end what I learned was this... it's perfectly okay to not be okay. You'll acquire some haters after taking a strong stand as I did, and that just means that you are doing something right.

In conclusion, all I can say is that in my own experience and from research I've done, I have not come across anyone who really benefited from speaking their truth, as a whistleblower, myself included. As with myself, most live to regret doing what they did and the aftershocks that it caused. People will want to know your story, but none of them would trade places with you after they know it.

# Introduction

This book is a memoir. It reflects my present recollections of experiences over time. My memories are imperfect, but I am sharing them to the best of my ability to remember. Names and characteristics of those in the book have been changed, some events have been compressed, and some dialogue has been recreated.

# Preface

The first step in their plan was to keep us all separated; divide and conquer. Their second step was to only allow communication through the attorneys. Any information that I was supplied from either side, was always filtered through attorneys. This was a manipulated narrative. Their third step, was to make sure we lost our appeal, shutting down my ability to ever go after my father's estate again.

This attorney never amended the complaint and never made good on his promise to us that he would present the fraud. This same attorney was a politically connected, former county commissioner, eager to take your case just to make sure you lost your legal claim.

Three years later, I found the same attorney that lost my will contest written up in a news article which read... "Under similar circumstances, he loses a politically connected case, again confirming he is either terrible at his job, or he is on the take."

This lawyer clearly was losing too many cases at his firm. But he did file a lawsuit against the state unemployment board when his daughter's unemployment claim was denied. He sure showed up for work when his daughter was on the losing side of life, but it was okay for his clients (someone else's daughters) to suffer.

There is an old saying, "The fish only sees the bait and not the hook." I was the bait – that was for sure. And hook, line, and sinker, I sunk all the way to the bottom. What I still cannot get over to this day is how a Judge could rule on an appeal when he did not have all the files on the case. Seventy-four of our files were missing at the courthouse the day we lost the appeal. The judge ruled on that case, but it was not constitutionally correct. They were all playing a game with my life and even when I had all the proof I needed to win, no one showed up to do the job I hired them to do.

So, when y'all Google me know you're not getting the full story.

When asked what political party I am associated with I say the cocktail party. I really liked President Obama because I felt that he did the best for women in this country when it came to health insurance. President Trump is my favorite, and I am not here to fuel any arguments however, I will say that he was our last President in my mind. What came after was an insult. As a female we waited an eternity for a woman to break into the White House and I never saw our First Vice President and to me that is a slap in the face for every female who ever dreamed of that job opportunity.

People are not running for office; they are running for cover.

Now what I could not overcome was how a Judge ruled on an appeal when he did not have all the files on the case. Seventy-four files were missing from the courthouse. The judge can rule on that case, but it's not constitutionally correct. They were all playing a game with my life and even when I had the proof, no one showed up to make it correct.

My plan: You cannot hit a moving target. This time I have no lawyer to be my battering ram. Only my two most faithful companions, Ride and Die.

After all the convoluted stories the smoke cleared. This time it was a solo act.

There is a lot to be said about a cooling off period. This is how the comeback is greater than the setback part. I go from the bottom to the top and this time I am staying there. I found my voice. I was not ready to give up just yet. Write a book they said, it's going to change the world.

Up until this point I was playing it safe, doing that only protected everybody else.

# Prologue

hush mon·ey

/ˈhəSH ˈˌmənē/

noun

INFORMAL

1. money paid to someone to prevent them from disclosing embarrassing or discreditable information.

"he used it as hush money for his mistress."

Definitions from Oxford Languages[1] Google July 13, 2022

If you are not trying to catch the bad guys, it's probably because you are one. Or, you may have to become one to play their game. I'm going to be honest with you here and tell you that even though what I did was the right thing to do, it wasn't. Yes, many will applaud your efforts and tell you that you've done the right thing - to be a whistleblower that is, and to that I ask, "The right thing for whom?" The aftermath of being a whistleblower has had a severe impact on my life. You are nobody's hero, and there's nobody coming to save you. No, not even Erin Brockovich is coming after you with a lifeboat. You navigate alone. The only person who can save you is yourself.

One would think that by now, the lawyer, (the man responsible for

---

everything), should have been caught, held accountable and face disbarment. Yes, realistically that should have been the outcome. Publishing an entire book, and exposing this lawyer, his law firm, and their dirty deeds took me a long time. During that time, I had to continually relive the trauma I was put through. These high-powered lawyers ruined my life. Every time I re-read a chapter from my first publication it was like ripping a Band-Aid off a wound that wasn't healed. And it's hard to heal when those raw emotions constantly plague me. But if I did not write the accounting of what occurred, nothing could, or would change - not for me, and not for any of the other victims.

The whole point of publishing my first book, was to uncover and expose the lies and the betrayals of those closest to me and their high-powered law firm. I did this by becoming what they call a whistleblower. The dictionary defines a whistleblower as a person who informs on a person or organization engaged in an illicit activity. Since that first publication, no one's lifestyles have changed, even after I exposed their lies and deceit. Everyone who wronged me has gone on making their hefty salaries and living the high life. By contrast, by exposing them, I've risked everything, and have often asked myself, "If nothing comes of it all, did I end up in a worse situation than I was in before?" Maybe all I'll end up with are a few breadcrumbs and a lot of agony.

I've wondered how Koger's life has changed since he ended up with all the money that rightfully belonged to Gia and I. One thing I know is that my sibling's lifestyles are pretty much the same, so they didn't profit. The dirty lawyer had their hands tied, and that is exactly why I attempted to go after him in my own way.

**And, so here we are meeting up as a collective once again...**

# Chapter One

People have asked me over the years what was the hardest part of my journey?

My answer is that I went about it all alone. There was a lack of moral support and understanding from my sphere of influence. No matter how many times I tried to explain to people how it felt navigating this big world solo, nobody was able to wrap their head around all that I had been through.

And so, I decided to show them instead of talking about it. Lead by example because nobody really understood the trauma and mental anguish anyway. Besides, I always made it look easy, when in fact, I just never let them see me sweat.

There were a certain number of people who regarded me as though I was the problem. I was only a problem for Koger. Remember he did this to other people, other families, other legacies. Koger was making me the issue because I was the only one that was strong enough to call him out on his lies and deceit. When we met up, he met his match. I was disrupting his order of business. I showed him where he lost all his control. He no longer was going to be able to use my siblings as shields.

I was telling the entire world he was a thief. He did not scare me, and he did not intimidate me at all. I was the voice of the people who had no voice because he slit their throats. He was no longer going to be able to scheme his way into his top one hundred Forbes-family clients. This time he pressed his luck for the last time. If he thought I was going to allow him to continue to manipulate and extort my father's legacy, he was not a very astute man. I do not deal with manipulation very well. I think it is the coward's way into and out of encounters.

To realize that there is someone (that someone being me, Stella) spending every day of their life dedicated to taking down his corruption, must be unnerving to him. I was not going to let him break me. All I was doing was breaking free of his control and this is how I did it.

I had to find a way to transform all the energy within me into something positive, and once again, I turned to my spirituality for answers. I started over with just $20 in my pocket, two suitcases, my two yorkies and a cheerful outlook. How was I going to shift this energy around? I knew it was going to be a long, bumpy road ahead of me, but I decided to embrace every day that passed and find the joy in it.

If I continued to compare my new life with my old one, I would have probably jumped off the nearest bridge just out of despair. There was no time for a pity party, and negative energy was not going to serve me, so best to figure it all out while I had nothing but time on my hands. Besides, even bumpy roads had to lead to somewhere.

The best way I can describe how I felt is to ask you to think of a bird. The bird is a small, winged creature that flies about. That animal is flying off pure instinct. The tiny bird has a brain, and within his brain he thinks simply of, safety, security, and freedom. Those are the three top reasons any animal survives. On the spiritual side, the bird represents freedom; the air element and the opportunity to deliver news with rapid precision.

Writing a book is a solitary experience. I was flying by the seat of my pants, but I gained clarity within the silence.

I needed to stabilize myself and get moving to stay established and be successful. I invited abundance and prosperity into my life. I decided to count my blessings instead of complaining about insignificant issues. I established an "eye on the prize" attitude. I began lighting my abundance candle, and I started praying for the ability to focus and sustain.

Being single is a choice, but there are the friends who become your soul tribe - a surrogate family of sorts. But people are busy raising their own families, running their homes, and working their jobs. Having gone through this experience without much human interaction, I learned to run purely off instinct, just like the bird.

At that point in my life, I was living in Florida. My roommate was gravely ill and on Hospice care. I knew my time at the house I was at sharing would end soon. It was important that I refocused and change the course of my life quickly.

I looked through all the housing ad's and I scoured every job lead but I knew I could not stay in the area where I was living. I decided I needed to get on the road and head back up north. If I was going to make this work, it had to be right then and there. A friend suggested I try looking for a place on social media. I turned to Facebook, and I did find a place that day.

The following Monday, I started messaging a woman on the ad I found on Facebook for an apartment above a retail store in a rural area. The apartment was $750 a month, all in. I left messages almost begging her to give me the apartment sight unseen. She was not responding but I continued to pursue it. Finally, she contacted me and said it was indeed still available. I told her I was getting on the road and would be there Friday morning. Tuesday, I packed up my clothes. On Wednesday I sadly said goodbye to my roommate, grabbed my two Yorkies and started my trek north.

I drove for ten hours listening to the radio and calling friends to keep me awake. It was raining when I finally pulled over at the gas station in a nasty neighborhood where I came close to being robbed by a guy who was asking for money. I ran inside the gas station where there was a security guard. By the time I got out of the bathroom, grabbed a Monster drink, and checked out, the guy was luckily gone. Security had chased him off.

I continued driving through the rain and found there was no safe place to stop. I pulled into a truck stop thinking maybe I could sleep in my car for a couple of hours. The way that the truckers were looking at me in my Fuchsia-colored car made me uncomfortable, so I decided to get back on the highway. I kept driving, but I was getting very tired. I looked on my map's app for the next town that had more than one hotel. I got lucky found there was a college town that was coming up not too far ahead, so I stayed the course. I prayed out loud to Archangel Michael to cut any cords that were preventing me from finding a safe place to land and to clear the roads for my safe passage to the perfect place to stay for the night.

Exactly thirty minutes later I pulled off an exit and my eyes lit up like the Vegas strip. God had answered my prayers because there were at least eight hotels to choose from. I checked into one at 4am, got a few hours of sleep and a late check out.

I had a message from my future landlord saying it was OK to sign my lease on Friday morning. It was Thursday morning, and I still had a long way to go but should arrive by that evening.

I was starting over and going back up north in late fall meant that it was chilly. I had no warm clothes or a coat because I had left all my winter things in storage at my sister Gia's and when I left for Florida, I had no intention of ever coming back. So, I layered up the sweatshirts I had with me but when I finally arrived at my destination, I opened my car door and felt the chilly wind slap my face the way my mother used to slap me, when I was misbehaving!

As I drove past my new apartment, I felt lucky. It was above an art shop and there was a bar next door.

I checked into a hotel close by for the night, set the alarm for 6am and passed out. When I woke up the next morning, ready to meet the maintenance guy at 7am, the new landlord messaged me saying she had gone out of town and didn't have the lease ready, so I would have to make it work for the following day.

My gut turned inside out. All I wanted was to know that me and the dogs had a roof over our heads that night. I immediately called the front desk to keep my hotel room for another night but was told there were no rooms available.

Worst case scenario, we would have to sleep in the car that night. I called the property owner and begged her to let me have the apartment that day, lease, or no lease. She responded and said to meet the maintenance man in an hour at the apartment.

The maintenance guy had the lease with him, and I did get it signed that day. He directed me to a resale shop right next door to the apartment, where I found a couple winter coats for $5.00 each. He then pointed me down the street to a mattress shop, where I scored a floor model that was delivered two hours later. I then found a Walmart and bought the essentials. Back at the apartment, I lined up my bags of clothes around the perimeter of the living room. I had no furniture except the mattress.

Looking around, I suddenly felt lonely, isolated, and alone. Then, I took a second look around, and realized that in less than I week, I secured an affordable place to live where my two fur babies where not an issue. I also realized that I was in a better position than I had been in for quite some time. I felt like things were finally looking up and that maybe I had caught a break.

After expending all this energy, I slept for two days but I proved to myself once again that the universe will provide you with what you need. Therefore, anxiety is a useless emotion that only drains your energy. I realized that when I was thinking clearly and trusting the process, everything seemingly flowed with no resistance attached to it. I reminded myself that the present moment held all the power.

Whenever I started to get frazzled, I practiced what I learned in Yoga, centering myself and realigning my thoughts with current energies, manifesting my dreams into something to look forward to.

Coming back home allowed me to extend my state benefits as I looked for work. The "country folk" where genuinely nice to me.

They all knew that I was from the city and called me the "City Slicker." I wore my high heels everywhere I went, and everyone in town said that they never saw anything like it. I felt like Eva Gabor in Green Acres. It was fine. My lease was for six months, and I made the best out of living there.

I went to the forest preserve for walks, and I kept active. I reflected on how all of this started because of just one man – the corrupt attorney who changed my entire being. I spent six months in my country apartment. The country people stayed in their own lane. They rarely ventured from their borders to the big city. I told myself this lifestyle was fine and not permanent. It was like I was in town for a just a brief time, and if they don't mind me, I don't mind them. But it was a tough time for me.

There were so many times I had to go to the food bank to get packages of ramen noodle soup. When I did get a little bit of extra money, I made sure I replenished the items that I considered I had "borrowed" from the food bank.

One of my favorite recipes was Fish Stick soup. What was that exactly? Stella made this her "protein packed on a dime recipe" that consisted of frozen fish sticks added to my ramen noodle soup. The first time I tried to cook it, I burned it. However, after a while, I got the hang of it, and it turned out to be very tasty. I never learned how to cook very well, so that was a real achievement for me.

I would lay on the carpet with my laptop and work that way. Sometimes I would stand at the kitchen counter and work standing up all day. That was very annoying not to be able to sit down at all at a table, but I had to do what I had to do. I never had enough time, to sit around and complain about anything. Gratitude was the key that opened every door that mattered. I made friends, I made contacts, and eventually, I started looking for a place closer to my original hometown. With two Yorkies in tow, again it seemed like a daunting task.

I was secretly hoping I would be able to stay a bit longer in the country apartment, but the property owner would not extend my lease.

I once again started looking for apartments, but only qualified for one that was close to my former hometown. It was substandard housing. I had no choice, so I took it. If I would have had only one dog it would have been much easier but having two really lowered my chances of renting anywhere. I remember when I was looking for an apartment after the foreclosure Gia said, "It is going to be exceedingly difficult to get an apartment that will allow you to have two dogs."

Just the thought that she felt satisfied sabotaging me still bothered me, but I had no other choice but to move forward. I drove around the new apartment complex and felt disheartened when I saw the burglar bars on the windows. All I could think of is how my parents would have reacted to me living this way, but it was all I could afford for myself at the time. So, no matter what, I had to make the best of it.

Koger pushed me into poverty. I paid a guy and his brother $200, and they strapped my mattress on the roof of a van, packed up my clothes and started over in "da hood."

# Chapter Two

Even though the living conditions were substandard, I felt I was somewhat back on my feet after acting on the courage to return home. My roots were important to me, and felt I started turning my life around.

After years of being in the rebuilding stage, I'd basically established a new identity. I had no family support, and my friends where few. Yet, despite the lack of numbers, God made up for it, sending me what I call my earth angels.

Now that I was back in my hometown area, I had to come up with some sort of guide on how I would make staying put a reality.

First, I concentrated on the saying, "the strength of a mustard seed."

In other words, I had to first believe I could succeed. I started taking responsibility for my inner being and I did what I had to do to stay alive.

My transition back home was focused on happiness and not material gain.

One important lesson I have learned is when you want something badly enough that it starts controlling you, you have lost a grip on reality. At that point, you need to invite discipline and self-restraint back into your life.

I was not going to buy into any form of greed. I have tried to never want anything so badly that I allow it to control me. This is a noticeably big gift from the universe, a moral compass if you will, to keep us aligned with our frequencies.

I decided to take the scraps of paper lying around and with the knowledge I had, started getting busy writing an account of all that happened to me because of the deceit and greed of one powerful attorney.

The experience of writing my story was therapeutic. When I began writing, I couldn't believe I was writing a book about my life.

I had and still have a sad but true and very enlightening story to tell. I am now seeing my book purchased and read all over the world.

When I've talked to people about my former life and describe myself as an heiress to a small fortune, people say, "An heiress like Paris Hilton?"

I've answered, "Yes, but after her grandfather donated 97% of his money to charity, she too had to work hard for her success and make her own money." People always seemed surprised about that fact.

I hope my father is happy with my work, and I hope to see my family prosper after the truth comes out. There is no way the family business could be 100% successful without two of the owners being present. Possibly, they made a mistake, so why not offer forgiveness? Shouldn't we all do that? I want to. I am doing it. I never forgave the lawyer who did this to me. He accelerated the fight in me, then used me to serve his purpose.

I wrote my first book to enlighten people and expose the corruption within the legal system. I still feel as though it would have been just and fair since I did not win in court, to be compensated my share. But that is not what happened, so, let the world be their judge. In the end, I ultimately gave them the money. Going back and reliving the past I would not change it, I could not change it anyway. Whenever I thought that I had a right to my inheritance and they owed me the money, I would stop and block that thought. Instead, I would tell myself that I blessed my inheritance, and I gave it to them. I trusted that the universe knew what was best for me. Why would I want blood money anyway?

That money was worked hard for when my dad earned it, but now it was tainted at the hands of a dirty lawyer. Telling myself these things was how I got through the grief.

So, now I'm back and there's no more crying over spilled milk. I will make it either way. The angels were going to bless me in a new way, with prosperity, happiness, and abundance, and this time it would remain with me, and no one would take it away. I was determined to make it all on my own.

Enter career number two - book author. I am now the main player in my life. I knew that if I shared my story that I would be leaving my legacy behind. Any person on this planet could read, and benefit from my story and how the actions and legal issues that were brought against me were about a corrupt system.

I knew all along that I was taking a significant risk writing 'Shattered Windows.' Uncovering corruption is always a gutsy move and it was indeed risky. I figured that if they came after me, I could lose my life. But after what they put me through, it was a risk I believed was worth taking.

The Feds told me that they knew they were dealing with a broken system, but it was the only system they had. They were not going to let me step in and upset their apple cart. A note to self... when hiring a Class A lawyer, sue the FEDS! Their negligence and the part they played not acting on my claim was inexcusable.

In the 2006 Movie 'The Secret' they say that 92% of the money supply is controlled by 8% of the population. That means on average, 92% of Americans make under $77,000.00 a year - still a decent living. But what do you do when you want and need more? How do you make up for past losses and keep up with the status flow? Breaking through the glass ceiling as a single white female and realizing the government had you caught up in their matrix didn't make it very easy for me.

Life has changed. It is a multi-income stream world we live in now. If we are looking to break through to the middle class, it is not that far a climb if you think about it. But a woman has a difficult time breaking through the glass ceiling unless we advocate for ourselves. And that was exactly what I had to do. I did not fear my future, I was afraid the past would repeat itself.

# Chapter Three

One way I release my trapped emotions and energy, is to write my thoughts down in a journal. I love journaling. I have journals everywhere in a variety of distinctive styles. Whatever my mood is will determine which I write in. A handful of them are lined, and a few consist of only blank pages. But they are all waiting for me to get it out and write it down.

I also use a variety of pens, pencils, markers, and crayons. This way I incorporate various textures with my moods. I started journaling because I decided to go within and reflect. I needed to find a way to heal myself. What exactly was the root of my problem anyway? What was it that I could not numb with a substance but felt like that itch you could not scratch? Was it grief? Was it anger? I realized it was both and they equaled discord. So, what was the lesson there for me? Why couldn't I forgive this lawyer and what he did to me? People have asked me that question many times and I still cannot find a way to rationally answer them.

Besides journaling, I did meditation. I needed to feel my way through all this pain and suffering. It was the high road; it was the better choice and at the end of the day, I still needed to live my life. I genuinely wanted to be free of these feelings for the last time. I had accomplished so much and moved on, so what was eating away at me?

I ultimately realized it had to be the lawyer, the man behind the curtain, the pink elephant in every room of my mind. I thought about him and what he did to end my life as I knew it and pushed me into a life of grief and despair.

To be honest, I thought about him every day, and sometimes, several times throughout the day. I saw his face every time I thought of my circumstances. Every day when I woke up to my meager surroundings, I thought of him. My mounting credit card debt which led to maxed out credit were all caused by him. Thinking of him made me remember the loss and abandonment he caused.

I thought of him sitting in his overemphasized office, a large desk with a big high back leather chair, a landline phone with a cord and tons of extensions, a view of the river, a floor of assistants that would run to get him a Starbucks latte. There he would be sitting back working his "magic" in his office, not caring about any of the people whose lives he ruined while living a lie, knowing what he was doing was not legal, but smart enough to know how to get around the system. I thought about him leaving his office carrying a briefcase but stopping to put documents in a safe before driving to his expensive home in his Mercedes. I thought of him taking his wife to Europe, dressing her in the finest tailored clothes made from the finest of fabrics. And I thought of him with his family all out celebrating a special occasion at a high-end restaurant, and him picking up the tab for everyone.

I sat there for quite a while, thoughts of true crime stories creeping in and out of my head.

I believed it was only a matter of time before the darkness would come into light. But did I really think I could pull this off? Would I be able to get justice? Who else were his victims? Who else succumbed to his greed but either could not, or would not speak up? Would these people contact me?

I thought back to the day that I was standing in the lobby of his law firm. It was on a separate floor, away from the rest of the practice. The lobby occupied an entire floor of an upscale downtown office building. That was awfully expensive real estate. When I looked at the bigger picture, I realized it was a distraction. He was not going to allow anyone to see the bones of the operation. That was all kept quiet. There he was a prominent attorney with his supposed high-moral standard giving contemptible advice from his ivory tower.

When you have been in the business for as long as he claimed to be in his deposition, and was paid the top billing rate in the industry, why on God's green earth would he advise people to do what he advised my family to do?

After realizing the depth of the contemptible, damning advice by this attorney who shamefully profited, I have granted forgiveness to my siblings but never him. He will always bare the blame for orchestrating all of this. What kind of lawyer sits down with a family and advises them it was a clever idea to cut out two other members of a family? That would only make sense if the lawyer was going to profit nicely from it.

He concocted a story putting the blame on my father who was an elderly Alzheimer's dementia, type two diabetes patient. When he put the blame on my father, and took advantage of him, that was all the motivation I needed to save not only my own, but my father's legacy as well.

An honorable attorney would have offered us a "buy out," not cut two siblings out totally so there would be more for him to profit.

Who is this guy anyway? All my father's work, hard labor, fighting in WWII and his fate comes down to this guy? Nah I don't think so. Ever since this guy showed up on the scene I was abandoned by my family, poverty stricken, and impoverished. Nobody puts baby in the corner, right? Speak now or forever hold my peace I thought to myself. Koger was also very well protected, and no doubt knew how to wield the law, not only with a sword but with a shield. Still, I had to re-evaluate the universe and ask for protection from my higher power and source energy. If I was feeling inclined to do what I was about to do, I needed to know the universe had my back and would give me the protection I needed to make it out the other side alive. I knew I would make enemies publishing this book, but I knew I had to do it. He was a greedy lawyer who saw an opportunity, not once, but twice.

This was where I believe he had my sibling's hands tied. He was controlling everything. He did not just walk off the scene after my father died. To this day, his name is still on the corporate paperwork for my father's business.

He knew when he wrote the estate plan there was going to be a will contest, so he set them up to pay for his ongoing legal defense, he double dipped. Why are they paying for this when it very clearly all rests on his shoulders? Koger needs be caught, and then be used as an example of legal negligence.

Why did the FBI say to me "If you know what is good for you, you will keep your mouth shut" and then two weeks later I suffered a MOB attack. It's because they were in it with him, in it to win it. That's called collusion by the way.

I guess someone upstairs felt I was the person needed to fill this role, so I took the bull by the horns and said, "Let's ride." I had to work smarter, not harder. Since he did not want anyone to know what he did, I was going to have to uncover everything he did. If the world was going to be my judge, I needed to publish the proof. There was the answer, the ace in my back pocket.

People say, "I am going to retire and move to Florida." Well in my opinion, which is exactly what Florida is, a retirement zone. That was why I needed to come back to my home state. I loved the time I spent at the beach. I believe salt water is an amazing health cure. Salt, I've heard is, "sweat, sea, tears." The three ways to use salt water to cleanse your aura.

And so, I needed to return to an area where I knew I was an expert in my field and had the opportunity to thrive. At this point I was in credit card debt, and still making monthly payments to my last attorney. And then it hit me like a ton of bricks. Why am I paying an attorney who failed to make good on his retainer letter? He promised to expose and present the fraud, but he never did it, so he technically was in breach of contract. I blessed, blocked, and released that off me. He did not see one more dime of mine.

I looked around at my new studio apartment. My box spring and mattress sat on the floor, no frame. I immediately told myself I was getting a bed frame. I should not sleep on the floor. I thought to myself, "If this is a metamorphosis, I am the caterpillar in the womb. It's springtime, and change is in the air." I was going through a change, and change is good. I deserved a proper living arrangement. I bought a table from Ikea, a high-back-office chair, and a corner shelf unit. One more chair from Hobby Lobby to put in front of my mirror so I could do my make-up and self-care rituals. I felt better – like things were looking up, but it was frustrating. I kept longing for a new life, but the reality was, he cost me my old one. I knew the universe was in control, so what was the hold up? What did I have to do to prove to the universe that I was worthy of happiness? Did the universe sign me up for this task because they knew I could stick it out, I could be the one to oversee it? Should I rely on luck or talent?

# Chapter Four

I was not going to waste my expensive education, or years of knowledge and experience in the business that my parents gifted me, so I leaned toward my talent, all the while praying for a lucky break. They say God laughs at us when we make our own plans, because he already has our plans all laid out. I had to think about it realistically. My first thought was, do not do it. In the long run, it would save a lot of people's lives and livelihoods, but it could cost you everything and the climb back up to the top would be a long, grueling one. Most people give up, or self-destruct along the way.

I wanted to know the whole truth and unless I went down the path that I did, I would not have found out the truth. But the reality, the aftermath of me taking down an entire organization of white-collar crime, I do not recommend. Most people would have given up when met with the same extreme amount of resistance that I was faced with.

All I pictured was Koger behind a big dam. He was doing his best to hold back the water. Could I, together with my team of angels bust that dam down? I had nothing but time and all the motivation a girl could ever need to make it happen. I thought, the truth shall set you free. My first inclination was to use my anger as fuel.

We are taught to suppress our anger. It's a bad feeling, and uncomfortable for most of us to act on. But how could I continue to suppress this emotion? So, I decided to lean into it. Anger to me felt like fuel to my inner fire. I needed to move forward with writing the book and exposing the corruption.

At this point, I remained under a federal court order, and I was living my life with restrictions. I was not necessarily hiding from the world, it felt more like I was protecting my energies. So, I had to "be ready" when the opportunity presented itself to me. I was going through an awakening, I had to turn this anger into a positive result.

What would come of this? Going down this road will I stumble upon a bridge that could lead to a healing for the family? We were raised to stick together, as a family unit but they ran. Why would they do that? I kept going back to the same reason. The third-party influence. The lawyer. The stranger who knew nothing about us but took everything from us. He was the Tarot's three of swords to me – the person who brought hurt, and pain. That realization convinced me they needed to be free from Koger, his control and influence. Pulling those three swords out of the heart was going to be a painfully long process, but as we all know, time heals all wounds. If the pen is truly mightier than the sword, then in the end of all this chaos would be worth it ten times over.

I had all the proof. The question was how I going to turn all of it into a positive, tipping the scales to my advantage? I told myself I was not going to be mad; I was going to be motivated. But I had to remind myself that I could not control everything so was it worth the risk? My grandma would say, "Procrastination is a sin, so get to work young lady." I opened my computer and started typing my story.

# Chapter One...

I understand people might want to look up to me for the courage that I showed in facing the corruption but, in the end, it truly was not worth it. You are better off having a "New York state of mind", just looking down and looking away. If you have the money and/or financial and moral support, then maybe being a whistleblower will work out for you. But at the same time, you will suffer both mentally and financially. You must be able to win the mental Olympics.

I had planned to win the gold medal. But when you are financially down and out, and mentally worn out, it is near impossible. You are not going to get the acknowledgment, or the gratification you think will come with what you are doing. What you will get is a handful of people saying your story is just a trauma dump. I would recommend saving yourself. I lived through it all and becoming reestablished at life has been incredibly hard.

I set up my laptop, a printer, and a lamp on my new table. Now I could sit at my table and work to build back my business. I was well on my way. Writing the memoir would be my second job. It was not a paying job but at the same time I had no issues showing up for it. The bills I still needed to pay because they come every thirty days. I would still work at building my own company, selling the same product lines that I had trained on since I was little girl.

I disliked thinking about being in competition with my siblings every day. I knew my father perfected his craft and without a doubt had the number one bestselling product available, and here I was competing with it all so that I could keep a roof over my head.

It turned my stomach every day. Of course, I made sure that the products I sold were of good quality, but I always felt cheated that I was banned from selling products that came with my birth right.

I was humiliated once after my return to my home state, running into a high school classmate at the grocery store. She told me she had my father's products in her home and how happy she was that he had invented them because she loved them but at the same time was very sad hearing that I was down and out. I ended up acting like I had no idea what she was talking about. Obviously, she "thought" she was aware of my story.

I told myself right then, that there was no way someone was going to assume something about me and talk to me like that in public, without knowing the real story. So, I went to work telling my truth.

People were going to hear the truth. People knew my father and what they did know about him, they all loved. If my father had an enemy, I never knew it. He was a good man with a heart of gold. The only people who had a beef with him were people who took advantage of his kindness because he reminded them at every encounter, "First time shame on you, second time shame on me."

I kept working hard on my business. I reached out to all my former clients to let them know I was still in the game. I placed ads on all my social media sites and once a week I picked a topic to do a podcast that is very successful. But my emotions would go up and down like an elevator at this point.

I was so grateful to finally have the few things I had, but sometimes I wanted to crawl up and die. I couldn't get over the fact that my brother was driving around town in a Ferrari while I was living the in subsidized housing. The apartment I called home was a dangerous place to live. There were people sleeping in the hallways of my apartment and the air always smelled like dope and sweat. I feared for my life taking the dogs out every day. I never invited anyone to visit me.

I had to call in Code Enforcement because my upstairs neighbor was breeding dogs and urine was seeping from his apartment into mine through the ceiling.

I walked over water puddles in the laundry room, risking electrocution just to do my laundry. The slumlord knew his way around the legal loopholes, so any service request went ignored and then the office staff erased them off the computer system, so there was never any request stored. I did take screenshots and emailed them to the leasing office and the property owner, I never received a response.

Their apartment website did not live up to what it advertised, so I reported false advertising to the state, but nothing was done about that. The hot tub reported to be on the property had not worked in six years. I reported false advertising to the Attorney General's office. It was one of the reasons why I choose that property v. competing properties. I reported about how the cost of the laundry was off by half the price, and how there was no additional security as they stated they offered.

The size of the complex was approximately eight hundred units. That was way too many people who were paying for amenities that they were not receiving per the contract agreement. A residential lease is a legal and binding agreement. It does go both ways. The property owner must perform to the standards and the degree of what they state they are offering.
Since there was nothing, they would do for me I took the next available option and wrote negative reviews everywhere I could. If you see something say something. They finally agreed to fix the ceiling after two and a half months, but I could no longer put myself through the mental anguish of living there. I had to manifest something better, I deserved it. I tried my best to make the best of it, but then again, it was time to pull the plug.

I once again turned to a Psychic hotline. I called and said, "I gave a 60-day notice to my apartment landlord. I'm due to move out and I need to find new place today. Where do you see me living next?" Psychic #0572 said, "Get in your car drive one mile north and it will be to your left."

I signed a new lease there that day. My apartment number was 111. For those of you who are not familiar, that is an Angel number that signifies protection.

I took it as a sign from the universe and I knew I was at the right place at the right time. I had lived in that area for over ten years, but I never noticed that apartment complex in all that time. I rented a truck, packed up my few belongings and moved into a new and better place.

The slumlord sued me in county court for eviction and I counter sued for damages. They broke their contract when they never supplied me the services agreed to in our contract. My pro bono lawyer provided by the county stepped up and interpreted the law on my behalf. Correct, I could not be sued for eviction because I served my property owner properly and I had substantial reasons for vacating my apartment. Because I counter sued the property owner for damages and moving costs the judge proceeding over our case transferred it across the hall to small claims court.

After over a year, the judge ordered me to pay the slumlord's legal fees, but I was awarded a refund to my account on over charges. The property owner charged me for a pet deposit, a pet fee, and pet rent - one charge too many. Because I represented myself pro-se and we held a bench trial, the judge did not grant my request to receive damages. She said, "Hypothetically, even though your freezer shelves are broken, it's cosmetic, the landlord still supplied a freezer."

I answered, "What? No, it is only in working condition if it's working and serving its purpose. If the handles and shelves are broken, it does not matter if it stays cold, it is still broken and not in working order. And yes, I have a problem paying for things that don't work properly."

But here we go again, history repeats itself for me because Pro Se is No Say... The eviction portion ultimately was dropped because I gave proper notice, but that did not stop them from obtaining a judgement against me. The judge sided in the slumlord's favor. Who elected this lady to the bench, I wondered?

That female judge knew the hardship the property owner put me through. I even had Code Enforcement come in and testify on behalf of the unhealthy environment they had me existing in, and she turned around and granted them a judgement against me. She had apparently lost touch with her feminine side. Maybe she thrived on a power trip sitting up on her throne and looking down at me, the little guy.

Even after I reported back to all the governing authorities, they still looked the other way. I kept asking myself, is it just THIS state or does the entire country operate like this? How does it work in other parts of the country? How could the system be this unjust?

The wheels in my head started turning. I took it one step further. At this point I was still a licensed Real Estate Broker, so I did what I signed up to do - monitor fair housing laws. I reported it to the state. They investigated on my behalf. It took eighteen months for all the paperwork to be reviewed and in the end, it showed I was right, and I knew my rights. Yes, they overcharged me, and they did discriminate against me. They charged me as a single white female for services and amenities they did not charge other minorities, so it was a moot point. I only lived there for five months, the entire process of leaving took over eighteen months to finalize. But, in the end I did win, sort of. I was justified in my actions although it drained me and the county of resources all because one man would not do the right thing by his paying renter.

Once again, I learned a little more about the law, and although I never went to law school, I felt like I earned a degree.

The state was able to offset the judgement with the fees they over charged me so ultimately my arduous work did pay off there. For people who think single white females are not discriminated against, I had just proved that they were, because I was one of them. They overcharged me because they figured if you could afford two Yorkies, you can afford to pay more. That is how they got around charging me a higher rent. They did charge me illegally for pet fees. After the state investigation, it was revealed that the Caucasian man across the hall paid only a pet fee and pet rent. The Hispanic lady next door with the Pitbull never paid anything for her pet, and neither did the Black couple upstairs who had never registered their two Pit Bulls or their Rottweiler. The property owner looked the other way for other minorities. Many people might call it reverse discrimination, but I call it straight out discrimination. Reversing discrimination is when you can do something about it and create change from it.

# Chapter Five

I was fascinated by the fact my apartment was an angel number.
What exactly is an angel number? It is an alignment with numbers.
They say 1111 is a portal to the angels. When you see 11:11 on the
clock, that is referred to as the "magic minute" - the minute you
whisper your prayer to the angels, and they hear you. And there is a
bonus - it comes around twice a day, every day!!

My apartment number was 111 - one for health, one for wealth,
one for peace. It was a suitable one bedroom with a good-sized
walk-in closet. No balcony or patio, only a view of license plates
out my window on car bumpers.

The living room was my office and where a couch and tv should be,
was an IKEA room divider and a plastic bin sanctuary. The storage
bins were my furniture. I lived out of them now. I could not afford
furniture, so I made the best of it and promised myself that
eventually I was going to have the things replaced that were taken
away from me and the universe would give me something even
better.

My desk faced the wall adjacent to the stairwell and the mailboxes.
I wish I had a dollar for every time a delivery person rang the bell.
It is still better than where I came from, but nowhere near where I
was going. Eighteen months since I left my house and five moves
later, I felt a sense of calm come over me.

I needed a creative outlet. I was craving fun and something I lost
that I needed back. I was not going to spend my entire existence

writing a book and working. I channeled my "inner goddess" and started looking for a dance class.

Even though I knew I was eventually going to find a way to catch this unethical attorney, I was not going to let opportunities for creative fun pass me by. I learned that lesson the absolute hard way. This time it was going to be on my terms. I started taking back control and paid myself first with joy.

So, I considered what kind of dance class would be fun and exciting for me? I tried Ariel Yoga but one large bruise on my thigh and I was done! Barre Yoga was next. I enjoyed the class when the instructor was present, which was less frequent than her absences.A red flag from the universe. I already did the pole series, and I would need a partner for Salsa. What else was there? "Alexa what dance can you learn and be solo and sexy?"

I chose to join a Burlesque class. Yes, it was as fun as it sounds. We would all meet up for ninety minutes a class, once a week. We would get all dressed up in our dance clothes wearing full blown makeup, wigs and all the bling we could shimmy. We would learn a dance routine each session. At the end of the session, we could choose to participate in a class performance - a recital of sorts. They would showcase many choreographed numbers. Some were solo, then they had a few duos and the majority of the dances where full class numbers.

I did one show. I was a stage kitten. A stage kitten performs in class numbers and goes up after each performance to pick up the props from the previous numbers. It was a blast. My stage name was 'The Dancing Doll'.

Originally, I put the name 'Miss Understood' on my sign-up sheet but was eighty-sixed by the teacher whose name was 'Miss Behaving.'

I could always do the splits, so at the end of the group number I shot right down like it was nothing and the whole crowd went, "WHOAAAAAAAAAAAAAAAA."

Each week I would experiment with different costumes and themes. Scarves, hats, and bejeweled tassels were amongst the favorites of the group. Dance is an important part of our lives. When we dance, we create movement with our bodies and in turn can release trapped emotions. Shakira said it best, "Hips don't lie."

Trauma can take up residence in various parts of the body, and for me it was in my hips. Shake your hips and unleash trapped emotions, otherwise we will be walking the path of disease instead of wellness. I decided to start going to the work-out room at my apartment complex and working out in various ways in addition to the dance troupe. I am feeling good keeping up with my self-care responsibilities and releasing pent up tension at the same time.

# Chapter Six

I did not know anyone who wrote and published a book, so I put it out into the universe and asked for help. The answer came a few days after, when a local newsletter from the library hit my mailbox. It was the answer I was asking for, "Come and join our writers' group. We meet the second Monday of each month."

I signed up that very day. I walked in with my notebook and sat down. There was only one other woman sitting at the tables.

"Are you here for the writers group?" she said. "I am. I am new, first time here." I replied. "You are here way too early. Come and fill out the new member forms and once we get started you will see how we operate."

I walked over very nervously and took the forms. I sat down and laid out my notebook and pen and started filling them out. By the time I finished I looked around the room and every seat had been filled. I sat there quietly absorbing all the information that was sent my way. They had an agenda that was the same protocol for every meeting. One person started with their name and why they came to the meeting. Then they went around the room and each one of us spoke one by one. As I listened to each person speak, I was getting more and more nervous. What was I going to say when it was my turn? If I say that I was writing a book about corruption and ousting the MOB, their reactions will surely differ. I felt invested in this class and I wanted to stay, so I played it cool. I was terrified they would be scared off and not want to help me, so I went general. "Hi, my name is Stella, and I am writing a memoir about my life and how I was caught up in the justice system," I said, as I felt a sigh of relief come over me.

I guess that didn't sound too out of the ordinary to them. There was a young lady who was writing a science fiction book, about a magician with one hand. Another lady was writing a story about Cowboys and Indians, and then there was the most interesting young man who was writing a comic book. Month after month we would meet up in the large conference room and two people from our group would read two chapters from their book. The rest of us would make notes on our copies that were given to us from the guest readers, and we would proofread and critique each other. I loved it. I never missed a class.

After about four months people asked me when I was going to be ready to share chapters from the book that I was writing. They caught me off guard with this. "I should be ready in about two months." I replied.

Fred, who was the facilitator, replied, "You don't have to convince yourself that you're an author you know. You are here now and there is nothing more to prove. We can only help you with your writing if you start sharing what you got. I will put you down for the next meeting. Bring two chapters."

"Gotcha, I will be here and thank you so much."

I wanted to run out of there go home jump into my bed and pull the covers over my head. I was scared. The reason why, was because guess who the universe sat me next to in class? A former FBI agent.

Whenever asked about my experience with the FBI, I always say the same thing "FBI stands for Forget About It." Unless they are scoring money off you, then you can go sleep with the fishes. I felt that the universe was again playing a cruel joke on me. He was writing stories about his time as a former FBI agent.

At first, I thought, "I am not going to say a word to this guy." All I needed was for him to go start talking to his buddies about what was going on, and there goes my story. I decided to sit back and keep my mouth shut and open my ears, listen, and learn. If your mouth is open, then you can't learn, so I played it smart and I was tactical. I was as quiet as a mouse taking a piss on a piece of cotton. Learn from everything he had to offer, I told myself. Up until that point, I was moving in silence.

He shared chapter after chapter about his life's career working for the feds. And each time the players changed names, but the outcome was the same. Once again, they needed to provide a paycheck for themselves and that meant bringing in the busts and seizing money to fund their departments. They never thought anything about the families or the victims. Only that they were doing their job to keep their job. Completely emotionless as they worked. He talked about how they seized all kinds of items that translated into money for the department and point blank admitted all they cared about was the money.

The FBI works with the bad guys, and they look the other way for the most part because they know they are not going to stop all the bad guys, but they will be satisfied with the bread crumbing of it all.

So, I asked myself what was the lesson for me here? What was I supposed to learn from this? I needed to learn both sides. If the universe put me smack dab next to an FBI agent, it was probably because I needed to learn more about the system.

What was I missing? Finally, I knew what it was. Koger's role in it. Why he did what he did, and the way he did it, for a living. He was and is the hired gun. Pay to play politics. He's an associate to the MOB who essentially can be called a Capo in his own wheelhouse. He was used the same as he poached his victims. In the rulebook of the Mafia, an associate is one who works with the mobsters but has not taken the vow of Omertà which is the vow of silence.

Maybe he did not like being in that position. Maybe there was a part of him that did not want to be a part of all the corruption. I had no idea the pressure he was put under to collect money from clients. All I knew was that he would be thinking, "I wish she would shut the hell up," once my book was published.

This is a dog-eat-dog world, and our job is to eat or be eaten. Therefore, I must recommend keeping your mouth shut. The authorities are very much a part of keeping the mafia going because they know it is bigger than them and they can't totally stop it. Just the same as me stopping the corruption. All that the authorities can do is be satisfied with the breadcrumbs. They can be an annoyance to the system, but they are never going to be able to stop it or take them down.

Koger was a part of this system. He was a partner in a law firm. He did not own the whole practice. Someone had to be the fall guy. When Koger showed up at the deposition with a bodyguard, was the bodyguard there to protect him or the law firm? I think he was there to be a heavy.

I went home after that class feeling exhausted and decided to not think about it so much. After all I was there learning the writing process and I did need beta readers, so it was time for me to start speaking my truth.

Connecting with that writer's group was the smartest thing I did in helping myself publish my first book. They taught me so much about the process. A beta reader is someone who will read your book, and in this case, it was those twelve people who listened to you read two chapters at a time, and then give their feedback - the good, the bad, and the ugly.

So, I was able to get a perspective about how my book was going to be received and, also if I was going to be able to keep the reader engaged. We discussed the importance of having a professional book cover designed and how to obtain a publisher. We talked about editing, hiring an editor, marketing, royalties, and self-publishing.

That same night, I woke up at about 3am and felt something crawling on my leg. I turned the lights on and flicked something off me. Splat it went against the wall and fell onto the carpet. All I could see was that it was black. I put my glasses on and there it was a cockroach. Holy mother of God. I ran to get my vacuum and sucked it up quickly. I was so disgusted. I sat down on my bed and thought to myself, "Now what?"

I turned my head to the left and there were two more crawling up my wall. After taking a picture of them with my phone, I sucked those up with the vacuum and went straight out to the trash. I slept with the lights on all night long. I was terrified of my living situation. I tossed and turned all night waiting for the leasing office to open at 9am when I would go down there and show them the photos of the disgusting place I lived in.

I am not going to lie, I started thinking whether the FBI was literally planting bugs in my apartment. They do say homes gets "bugged" right? They don't call them bugs for nothing! Maybe they implanted microphones in the roaches? I had lived there for a year, and I never saw them before so what gives now? I did not have anything to hide but Koger did. I was positive they had kept tabs on me and maybe they wanted to know more since I was good at keeping a low profile. Then I told myself that I was just being paranoid and put a pin in it.

After all I had accomplished in my life I was now living with the roaches, I had sunk to a whole new level of low. The anger that I felt remained unresolved because of how I was forced to give up the best years of my life. There I was in the prime of life, trying to establish myself in the industry I knew so well, but just getting by enough to keep a roof full of bugs over my head.

And this is what I am saying... I know people want to hear me say it was worth it; to stand up for yourself. But that would be a bold face lie. It was never worth it, and no amount of money would be able to convince me otherwise.

I looked up the symbolism of the cockroach in the spiritual community. They say when a cockroach crosses your path it means you are a survivor. It is because they have been around since the dinosaurs, and you can't kill them. They can live up to 40 days without their heads. They will survive a nuclear war. Once again, the universe reminded me of exactly where I was - in survival mode. I was a survivor, and I was not going to give up.

# Chapter Seven

It's frustrating! It had been over ten years since my journey started and I can tell you that in the beginning of all of this, what I thought of law enforcement was just that, they were enforcers of the law. I previously thought that the Feds were out there after the bad guys all the time. And they were, but they were also in the business of concealing the truth. Concealing is not the same as lying. Nobody ever said anything, so it could not be held against them later. Like my dad used to say, "The fish wouldn't have been caught if he didn't open his mouth."

Unless of course they were all on the same team. Once again, we find HU$H MONEY. Can you really blame them? Wasn't Koger a husband and a father providing for his family? I was starting to work through my stymied trauma by realizing there were so many sides to the story.

Back to the writing group. I was still very hesitant on talking. The wheels kept turning in my mind and I became paranoid with the former FBI guy in our group. I had PTSD episodes constantly. If someone knocked on my door the dogs and I were set off.

The leasing office started spraying every month for the roaches. They knew that I had to be home and we had to have an appointment before they could enter. Once they entered, I packed up the dogs and put them outside. When the exterminator sprayed, we would leave for several hours to allow the application to dry. I specifically told the exterminator not to leave any sticky traps or bait because I feared my dogs would get into them and that would be a huge medical emergency and cost.

I ran into an old friend from high school walking down the street. We first met when I was fourteen and my dad took me to the mall to buy some clothes. He would take all us girls to this shop called Contempo Casuals. Because my father was in his sixties, my friend who worked there let him sit at the counter and eat a slice of pizza from Sbarro's that was just across the way. It was years since I spoke with her but after I ran into her so randomly, we started speaking again. She was 6' tall and had legs as long as the day. We used to discuss different episodes of Sex and the City, and she always wanted to me to channel my inner Carrie so I could score a Mr. Big. She claimed her spirit animal was a Giraffe and I could only giggle about that because for obvious reasons, it fit her. I called her French Fry because we made a pact, it was fries before guys.

Her dad was a retired English teacher, and she went to visit him almost every day. I asked her if he would mind being a beta reader for me and have a look at my manuscript and possibly offer me some pointers. He said he would be delighted to do it. He was bored sitting at home and in between doctor's visits he agreed to help me out if I would supply him with at least one red pen. I handed her the first two chapters and a red pen, happy to oblige.

It took about two weeks, and I received my first draft back with red pen marks all over it. Finally, my masterpiece was on its way to being published. I worked more and more on my book and there came the proof that my hard work was paying off. We kept this going for some time. She could see how hard I was working and invited me to a Madonna concert for a fun night out. I accepted the invite and we both gathered all our favorite 80's material girl gear. We went to the concert and people there were dressed up as different eras of Madonna.

Madonna did not get on stage until 11 pm so French Fry said her husband spotted us a hotel room off his corporate points right across from the theater. We laughed until the early hours of the morning and eventually passed out. When I woke up the next morning, I was in a hurry to get back home.

I ran out of the hotel room and down the street for coffee, grabbed a breakfast sandwich, hugged my friend goodbye, and took off back home. When I got to my door, I saw a card stuck in it that said the exterminator had been there. I was so angry. He knew he was not allowed entry into my apartment when I was not home because the dogs were left running around. I complained to the leasing office, but they didn't care. I was so mad at myself for going out and staying out and now look what happened the second I let my guard down.

Three months later the pandemic hit and now we are all stuck at home.

# Chapter Eight

I thought back to a time when I first met Julia who moved into the house next door. She threw a housewarming party, invited me and I went. While she gave me the nickel tour of her home, I noticed a wall of open cubes she used as shelves in the lower level arranged from floor to ceiling. Each cube had items symbolizing a part of her life. In one cube was a heart and a card from her husband and it showed they had strength and unity in their marriage. Another contained a teddy bear and a child's toy symbolizing their son and his childlike wonder. There was one cube that was completely empty. I stood there wondering about it. Well, she did just move in so maybe that one had not been unpacked yet. I decided to ask her.

"What are you putting in this one - the empty one," I pointed to it with my index finger.

"Oh, that one. It's going to remain empty," she said.

"Why?" I asked politely.

"That is the space that I use for allowing. I am letting the universe know that I always have space for new energy to enter my life," she explained.

I shook my head in wonderment and considered. From that moment on I realized how important it was to leave space in your life, a pause of sorts, to allow life to happen.
The year 2020 was a game changer for everyone. It was time for us to clean up our act as a collective. The world went through a cleansing. We needed it. Being in quarantine gave us all a time out.

Time to think and reinvent ourselves. It took the whole world to shut down in order rebuild. Quarantine was required for two and a half months and was suggested for much longer. Social distancing was a plus as we learned the gift of togetherness.

I refocused. My business, the one I worked on since 2011, was shut down. There was no work. At one point I felt like we were all going to die. If there was a time that I thought my family was going to reach out, it would have been then I thought. Nothing like a good apocalypse to bring a family closer together to heal old wounds. This is what my father prepared us for since he lived through The Great Depression. But nope, they never looked back. They left me for dead and it stayed that way.

My friends where not much help during the pandemic either. They had a hard time dealing with my PTSD. Some of them could not understand or relate to the trauma I had endured.

At times I felt like saying, "I am sorry that the version of me isn't lining up with your version of me, but this is my reality. This is who I have become, and I am not sorry."

I recalled the stories that my father told me about the Great Depression and how he prepared us to get through a situation like this. But still nothing. Nobody showed up in my life. I continued to work on my book and figured I would make good use of the time I had to myself.

I was used to people dropping off the radar for other reasons, like when they find out you dealt with the FBI, they would run for the hills.

Watching 'Schitt's Creek' helped pass the time and at the same time was very cathartic. I found that storyline to be very relatable, seeing that Alexis Rose and I both owned the same dress at one point.

Depending on the episode and the season, I could relate to each one of the characters and how the universe could take everything away at any moment. Of course, my thinking was that it could be replaced with something better.

I decided to start looking for publishers. When you are looking for a publisher, you need to have what is called a Query Letter. You look up what the category your book falls into and then you start sending out your Cover Letter with a Query Letter and sometimes the first three chapters of your book. I had all these things. I was not quite finished with my book since it was being proofread (slowly) by Frenchy's dad but, I was getting a head start on the process.

Sagittarius' are this way, over thinkers, always wanting to be ahead of everything, getting out in front of it. Months went by and I applied to thousands of agencies. Nobody was working due to the pandemic.

At first, I thought maybe I am not doing this correctly, so I had people review the packet I was sending out, and besides a few minor word changes and updates, I still received nothing back.

All I kept thinking was why would the universe bring me this far just to hit a brick wall. If Koger deceived his client(s), then there must be a way to get this story out into the universe. I took a minute to stop and breathe.

My two fur babies and I continued our daily walks. One day while walking, I noticed something on my female fur babies' paw. There was a growth between two of her nail pads. I wondered what it could be, so I started Googling it. Maybe an ingrown nail? She hadn't been clipped in a while because of the pandemic. I tried making an appointment at the veterinarian's office, but it was booked a couple weeks out. I did what I could do at home for her. I started soaking her paw in Epsom's salt, applying Neosporin, and then wrapping up her paw loosely with gauze. I put a baby sock over the bandage so she wouldn't bite at it. When the day of the appointment finally came, the Vet looked at her paw and highly recommended surgery. It sounded like it was going to be an easy surgery and he did not seem concerned about it at all, so I booked the operation and prayed it was all going to be okay. Surgery came and in addition to the growth on the paw, the doctor ended up pulling some teeth. Nevertheless, I picked up my girl and the bandages looked good. For two weeks I changed her bandages and cleaned her paw, and it appeared her paw healed nicely. Feeling pretty good that day, I took a break and sat outside. It was a beautiful, sunny day and I wanted to take advantage of the Vitamin D.

My phone rang and I saw that it was the veterinarian's office. My girl had cancer. I kept telling the doctor the biopsy was wrong and it had to be a mistake. I was in complete denial. Crying uncontrollably, I ran back into the apartment and picked up my baby. The follow-up appointment was heartbreaking. He told me point blank that the type of cancer she had was not curable and I needed to enjoy the time left I had with her.

Within two months she could not pick up her head or move it from side to side. She developed large tumors in her neck. The doctor told me to bring her in to have them drained. Our appointment was at two o'clock and emotionally, I wasn't sure how I was even going to drive there. When it was our turn, I placed her pet carrier on the metal table and let her poke her precious face out. I always called her my bag lady because she always slept in my purses, bags, and suitcases.

The doctor came in and examined all of her tumors. Sadly, he turned and told me he could not drain them and that it was time to put her down.                I fell apart right then and there. "Put her down? Why? You said you could drain these."

"Stella, I told you that your dog has a very aggressive form of cancer and there is no treatment that would cure it. I will let you take her home if you want to, or you can take her to another animal hospital for another opinion, but this dog will not survive more than a few more hours. If she where my pet, I would put an end to her pain and suffering."

That was literally the worst day of my life. I thought getting the phone call about my father dying was hard, this was worse.

I asked the Doctor "Are you sure there is nothing else we can do for her?"

"If there was anything I knew of, I would do it. She is in a lot of pain."

For anyone who has had to put a pet down. I am so very sorry for your loss. There are no words, and I am an author saying this; NO WORDS that can describe the pain you feel going through this process. One minute you are hugging your beloved pet and the next they lay there lifeless. I told myself after her death that I would never get another dog. It's way too painful. They are heart break hotel, they check in but never checkout.

I spoke with the doctor who told me that the type of cancer she had was possibly caused from pesticide exposure. The exterminator. She always laid on the floor, while her sibling always sat on the chairs, or the bed. She must have gotten into it, licked it, or got sprayed on. One way or another, the toxic chemicals got into her small system.

People asked me if I was going to sue the apartment complex about it and I said I could, but what good would it do? I cannot bring my dog back and they are going to deny it anyway. They would not even admit that they had roaches in the walls.

# Chapter Nine

It took me nine years to pay off all my bank debts. I worked at it consistently and sacrificed many good times just so I could muster up the minimum payment due. I figured I was tired of working for the banks money and I took control. I cleaned up all my finances and for the first time in a very long time, I could proudly say I was debt free.

None of the psychics on the hot line ever told me that my life would be reduced to roaches and rubble. I lost everything, but it made me realize that I could, and I have rebuilt my life. It felt good to usher in new energy. I would strive to become a best-selling author and continue to provide excellent service to my customers.

Once again, I sat down and was determined to finish my story. Every time I started writing, something seemed to stop me from making progress. Nothing was blasting through my writer's block, and I was getting frustrated.

They say people start writing memoirs around the age of fifty. This is when we start passing on our life lessons to the younger generations in hopes they will pick up on some of our life clues.

My day job was completely shut down and I had to figure out a way to get this book published with the time that I was given during the COVID19 crisis. I set out looking for an editor. With no extra money and scouring through ads online, I couldn't afford decent help. The memoir took me eight years to write but it felt like it was incomplete. It was not the masterpiece I wanted to put out into the world.

Then, it all came together in the eleventh hour. After applying at hundreds of agencies I said, screw it. "When opportunity doesn't knock on your door, build your own door."

Working on the book took a lot out of me and I was so excited to become a published author. It was a similar feeling to polishing a fine work of art. There is much to be said about the delays and all the time in between. I call it the cooling off period. Time to meditate on how you become older and wiser and more gracious. That bad things happen to good people but it's all relative and a perception of your state of mind. A delay is a way for the universe to catch up with the future.

I was one step further to completing a long-held dream of mine, and it was just days away. Not only was I ecstatic about my book being published, but I was also hopeful, that finally the truth will be revealed. I was elated.

# Chapter Ten

I received an email. The email was from my baby sister Gia. The email read, "Your things are in storage Unit #7177 (at this address), and you have until (this date) before you will be charged storage fees."

At first, I was not sure what to think of this. By this point, it had been years since Gia and I had exchanged any type of communication, and I felt it could be a set up.

My first thought was how I was going to approach this situation and avoid a confrontation with the family. I did not have an opportunity to recoup the items that I left behind from Gia's warehouse when I was kicked out, of her house. Remember I only had $20 in my pocket and two suitcases, and I left there thinking I was never going back. Since I did not have the resources to move my things into storage, apparently Gia did, and had everything stored in her warehouse moved into Unit #7177.

I wondered if somewhere inside utilizing my woman's intuition, I somehow knew I would one day be given the chance to recover what I was forced to abandon? Is this the reason I relocated back up North? Was this what pulled me back in the direction of home? But there was something else to consider. Did I really need any of that stuff? It had already been there for years, and I did not miss it, so why should I put myself through the possibility of a family confrontation? Always forward never back, right?

I called my friend Sunshine. (Yes, that really is her name) Her mother took one look at this girl's sunny disposition and named her accordingly. Sunshine is a practical thinker. She thinks about situations in terms of energy exchanges. She's also strong – the most physically fit woman I know. She convinced me to go after my items. She also convinced me that it was a sign from the universe that I could manage retrieving those items now. She said to think of it as if my sister had watched over the items for safe keeping and now, it was time to return them back home to their rightful owner. So, I started thinking about it differently.

Sunshine agreed to go with me to retrieve the items just in case it was not copasetic. She drove over and hopped into the Barbie Jet (as we referred to my car), and we drove over to the storage unit. We pulled into the warehouse parking lot ready to use the baseball bats we brought with us just in case. After navigating through the maze, we finally found Unit #7177. Sunshine quick like a cat, playfully slithered up, over and in between some stacked items. Reaching down and around into a desk drawer that was tossed about, she grabbed with one hand a file that looked interesting amongst some other miscellaneous files. She handed it to me after she crawled out from under the pile. The one file just happened to be my legal paperwork which contained the evidence (the most important file of my life) that I needed for my book.

She handed it over to me asking, "Does any of this mean anything to you?"

I replied, "These are the most important files that could have ever been returned to me." I showed her why.

Since the lawyer was able to convince a "select few" individuals that his work on my father's estate plan was legitimate, I was about to turn the tables on him. The judge could only rule on the evidence presented in court, but none of this evidence was ever presented in front of the judge.

The next, best common-sense move was to present that evidence in my memoir 'Shattered Windows'. Now, it would be in the "People's Court" - the court of public opinion. It was no different than from how Monica Lewinsky lived because she saved the dress, I thought to myself. Maybe the saying "Common sense isn't that common" came from a moment of clarity such as this.

Immediately following, I concluded that I was never going to win in court. He was letting the clock run out the entire time in his corrupt wheelhouse.

Koger had me buried in litigation, running me into the ground with running my butt back and forth into court. But still I dodged every bullet. There was no justice to be had in the justice system. Now I had to write the book and publish it. The people who were meant to find it will. It is energy. I think people should know he is a crook. Nobody should be involved in any kind of dealings with his guy. He's a fraud through and through. He didn't think I could do anything about what he did to me. I was about to prove him wrong.

I am pulling an Abe Lincoln here "You can fool all the people some of the time, and some of the people all the time, but you cannot fool all the people all the time."

I am also stating my case to the universe. "This job is way too big for Stella alone." I felt the need to release it all out there and finally take the pressure off just me, knowing this is going on. It's way too big of an issue to overlook.

There is no argument when you are stating the facts. I had struck gold via Sunshine on my initial search. I was sure Gia had no idea what was in that drawer of files. I quickly secured the files in my car and went back to delve into my other items.

In the unit stood my old king-size mattress. That bed saw more sex than I did. I couldn't remember what I had paid for it – back when I could afford a good mattress. It was the most comfortable mattress I've ever slept on. I realized I really missed that mattress from my old life. It had a pillow top on it that hugged you in all the right places and an energy field around it that sucked you in. My ironing board was in there, clothes hamper with the dirty laundry still in it, a pile of old shoes, and a Dior boot box. Everything was haphazardly thrown around. I did find my snow boots, which were still in the box, and in good condition. Sadly, the wooden desk from Marshall Fields that my father had given me was turned sideways, the drawers all broken. There was a lamp with a now broken glass shade and bag with my fur comforter, bed linens and pillows. Valuable items like my treadmill, my marble dining table, and my tower computer were in there. And the wooden jewelry box that my dad bought me years ago from Montgomery Ward.

Sunshine looked at me and said "You're going to need help moving all of this. As strong as I am, I can't move that marble dining room table over there, or that heavy granite desktop and I am pretty sure it's not going to fit into your trunk."

I returned the look and said, "I agree, I wonder how many workers from the factory it took to throw all my stuff in here without even a care?"

The granite top to my desk and the marble table were probably 400 pounds each. Care was not taken when those things were moved into the warehouse judging by the way they were dumped in there it screamed "I despise you."

I grabbed a few things that I could fit into my trunk including a few small picture frames and cooking utensils and we drove off.

I had to move the treadmill out first if I wanted to make room to rummage through the rest. I called my friend Frenchy. "You by any chance need a treadmill?" Frenchy was used to me calling and asking random questions out of thin air.

"Of course, we could use one, what's up? "

Her husband met me back at the storage unit. The treadmill I paid $4,000.00 now had a new home and once again was serving a purpose. Since she did have a house, she also took the shovels, water hoses, and purple Hunter rain boots still in the box.

I had a tiny apartment, and I could fit some of the items but how was I going to move all of it and where was I going to put it all?

I called Angelo. He looked like Tony Soprano. He was one of my old customers who married a high school friend of mine. I explained what my situation was and that I only had a couple of days remaining to get the items cleared out. I told him what was left in the unit, and he agreed to help me. He told me to call his brother and gave me his white cargo van to use the next day. It felt like Santa came with some of his elves and his sleigh. It took two days of going back and forth to sort through all the chaos. I saved what I thought I could fit back at my apartment.

Unfortunately, the vintage Ms. Pacman arcade game would not be going home with me. When I was a kid, we would go to a discount department store called Venture. I loved buying Keds sneakers there because you could get them without the blue label at a discount. They had a Ms. Pacman machine in the café. I would line up all the quarters my dad gave me – maybe five or six at a time. I could make her have the baby three times. I was awesome at it. My father purchased me a Ms. Pacman arcade game of my own when I was in my late teens. It sat in his living room for years. When I moved into my first home, I brought it with me. I remember moving it and wanting that machine to have a special place. When I was looking around the storage unit, I realized it was nowhere to be found. I thought maybe my sister was letting the niece and nephew use it, and if that was the case, I was OK with that.

Angelo let me bring everything to his warehouse, and I stored the items on the back shelves that he was not using. I told him I would come by from time to time and retrieve some of the items as I made room in my apartment.

As the months went by, whenever I went to the warehouse to pick up some of my things stored there, I was never able to access any of it because Angelo had moved everything way up to the very top shelves. I forfeited some agreed-upon items to him as storage fees, but when the day came to finally gather what was left of my things, it was slim pickings. He helped himself to what he wanted – mostly the more valuable stuff. I could not continue crying over spilt milk. I had moved five times during the prior eighteen months, so part of this was on me.

Frenchy helped me book a storage unit. This time it was a very small space and much more organized and manageable. I took the remnants of what was left and decided to move on.

The best, last item belonging to me, was the 'Yellow Car," aka "The Bumble Bee." The Monte Carlo was still parked at Gia's warehouse. There was a ratty old car tarp with a brick on top of the windshield holding what was left of it down. A quick once over and I noticed a new dent in the driver's side fender. I wondered how many times she might have thought about selling it but then backed herself up realizing that would be grand theft auto. I decided to overlook the new dent and express gratitude that the universe brought the last car my father bought for me back home where she belonged. "Queen Bee", was back like a long-lost BFF.

I was able to get the Monte Carlo towed to a quick lube. A few tweaks here and there and she was back up and running just like the day I drove her off the showroom floor. I was so happy to have my rusty but trusty Chevy back home with me. Not much felt like home anymore. But having this car back made me very happy, and at peace in my soul my true home.

# Chapter Eleven

I remember the day I got that car. I was working in real estate at the time, and I drove past the dealership that my brother-in-law was the general manger of. He and my sister were going through a divorce, and I wanted to stop by to see how he was doing. I ran into Kinko's across the street, made my copies of a contract that I needed and then drove over to visit him. When I pulled up to the dealership, I saw him standing outside talking to a couple of people. He looked disheveled and very thin. No doubt the stress of the divorce was taking a toll on him. I wanted to let him know that no matter what, we would always be family. I felt terrible that my sister was divorcing him after being married for almost twenty years. I always looked up to him and thought he was a great husband (although the Virgo in him made him a workaholic and that was an issue in their marriage.) He saw me pull up and get out of the car, and when I walked up to him, he told me to go inside and sit in his office. He would be in to speak with me after he finished up with his current customers.

I walked into the showroom and there she was. The brightest yellow Monte Carlo I ever saw, and I said to myself, "Stella wants her. Stella is going to take this beauty home."

Sitting at a desk nearby was my brother in law's brother who was a salesman at the dealership. He said, "Just look at that color yellow! It's really something, isn't it?"

I could hardly speak. It was love at first sight. I turned to him, and

I said, "I am going to buy it." "Oh my God, I have got to have this car!"

"I would too if I were you, and I wouldn't regret that decision. That's a great car."

I went and sat in my brother-in-law's office and waited for him to come back. When he finally came in and sat down at the desk, I asked him how he was doing. He told me he was beyond depressed, and he wished that the divorce was a bad dream. He wanted to stay my sister's husband and he loved her unconditionally. He was very distraught. I told him that no matter what, I had his back and that for over the two decades that he had been in our family, I cared about him, and we would always be family.

Then I finally said, "You know the yellow Monte Carlo out there? I want to buy it. Please write it up so I can take it home."

He responded, "Are you high? Did you smoke weed today?"

I said, "Weed? No! I did not. Why do you think that?"

He said, "Because I know you and I know that you cannot afford to buy that car."

I said, "That's not true. That car and I are soulmates, and we belong together! I think that the universe guided me here so I could drive her home. I feel connected to that car, and I say that is my car and I would like to buy her and drive her home. Please write her up!"

He said, "No way, and you need to leave right now."

I quickly responded, "Why do I need to leave, I am at a car dealership, and you sell cars, and I want that one, the big yellow two door coupe sitting on the showroom floor."

He yelled, "Stella, get out of here! You are not buying that car! You really can't afford it, so go home."

I saw that he was visibly upset so I left. I drove down the street and I spotted a Starbucks. Coffee. That's it. Coffee solves all problems I told myself. I went inside and ordered two cups. One for me and one for my brother-in-law.

I drove back to the dealership and once again saw him standing outside. He saw me walking up with the cardboard coffee tray, so he waved for me to go inside to his office. I went inside and dropped off the two cups of black coffee and ran out into the showroom, opened the car door, and sat inside my new ride.

The leather! Nothing smells as good as fresh leather in a new car. Everything about this car screamed, "STELLA!"

My brother-in-law came over. "I told you to go home," he said.

"And I told you that this is my car, and I am buying it and taking it home with me."

"You can't afford it." he repeated.

I said, "Yes, I can! I can afford to buy this car."

"How? You have no money." He replied.

"I can buy it and make payments. That's how I afford the car I am driving now." I replied.

He continued, "This car will be here for weeks. If you can come up with the funds, we'll talk. I'll tell you this though, no one is going to buy that car because yellow cars take forever to sell."

I replied, "I am not coming back in a few weeks, I am here now, and I am telling you that this is my car, and I am driving it home today. Stop messing around and let's get me financed, I have a trade in!"

I tried feeling hopeful while staring up at him. He motioned me to get into his office and so I went in there and sat down.

He picked up the phone and called Gia. "You need to tell Stella that she must leave my place of business. She came in here wanting to check on me and I do appreciate that kind gesture, but now she thinks that she can afford a new car, and I want her to leave so I can get back to work."

Gia laughed, "I think you know Stella like I know Stella, and she is not going to take orders from me, so have a good afternoon." She hung up the phone.

I said, "Told you, the universe is on my side."

He said, "I am calling your brother."

I said, "Good, tell him that I am buying a brand-new car and if he wants to, I can give him a ride in it."
Four hours went by, and it was push and pull the whole time. He wouldn't budge. I walked out of the dealership without my yellow car. I got into my black Hyundai that was in perfect condition by the way and drove around the block and entered in the service area of the dealership. I asked the young man behind the counter for a cardboard box. I told him I was trading in my car and that I needed to clean it out. He handed me a cardboard box and I told myself that the universe was giving me permission to act on this transaction. I opened the car doors, cleaned out the car, and thanked him as I put the keys up on the service counter.

I said, "Someone will be by shortly for those."

I walked back into the showroom and put the cardboard box on my brother in law's desk. "The service department has my Hyundai. I am ready to sign off on those loan papers now."

He looked at me and said, "You have been here all day. You cannot afford to buy this car. I called your father and asked him to come up here and to take you home since you can't afford to buy this car and you have tied up my entire day with your nonsense."

I looked out the showroom windows and there was my dad standing outside with my brother. I rolled my eyes and was like "what now?" with an attitude.

So, my dad walked in. "What is going on? You want to buy this car, but you have no money?"

While giving my brother-in-law a dirty look, I said, "It is true. I do want to buy this car, and I said I can make the payments."

My dad asked, "Did you even test drive it? How do you know that you want to buy it if you haven't taken it for a test drive?"

"I felt a connection with it. When I walked in, the car said, "I am all yours, take me home." Besides I know for sure this car is perfect for me. Just look at how good I look in it," I jumped into the front seat behind the steering wheel with my biggest smile.

My dad said to my brother-in-law, "Well, at least let her test drive it. I will go with her."

And just like that they opened the double glass doors on the showroom floor and rolled my car outside. I jumped in. My brother got in the back seat and my dad sat in the passenger seat. My dad told me to drive it around a little bit to see if I liked the way it drove. I got about fifty feet down the block turned the corner and headed back to the dealership and said, "See dad, it's perfect. I told you."

And within about two minutes we were right back in the dealership parking lot. I did not get out of the car.
My dad got out along with my brother and he turned to my brother-in-law and said, "Let her take it home, I will send a check for it in the morning."

And just like that she was all mine. Eight hours and three phone calls to my dad and it was official. I remember my dad telling me that was going to be the last car he ever bought for me, and it was. I still have the "Queen Bee" and she still runs as good as the day I brought her home. I will always be a Chevy gal.

# Chapter Twelve

The editor and I were in a surprisingly good space. I would eagerly await the next edited chapter, each time learning more about how to write and publish my own book correctly.

I thought about my part in all of this. I surely need to start taking accountability for everything now. My story is out there, and I am talking about corruption on the spiritual level. "Karma," I say, "I am the spiritual gangster quality control for the universe." If we meet up, we are eventually going to align for the good. The longer we procrastinate paying our toll to move on, we are getting our karma. So just know if this path resonates with you, let us continue. Purge out the negativity. Is it possible?

I could for example let Koger off the hook. Why keep it going? He knows what he did. I know what he did, and it was already done. My karma was to document it and then, let the claim go, allowing the universe to step in. To trust and observe. It is not my full-time job. My full-time job is to maintain my health, and that is my wealth. I am having an awakening. My soul's journey. I said to myself that I was transmuting this less than positive energy out of my mind along with the bad thoughts, poor decisions and Koger's corruption. I was evicting these thoughts because the energy was no longer serving me. If I did get any money from any of this, it would need to be clean money, and only I can do that for myself. I have written about my experiences and how I traveled the road back to home, but it is on my terms to be an author and to live out my life in peace. The less than positive energy could not live within me any longer. It had no power over me, and I vowed I would never give up on myself.

I sat and looked at a photo of my fur babies. I only had one now, but I thought to myself if I had to choose between one or the other, which one would I choose?

This was what that lawyer had to decide, correct? Which of the siblings would he kick out onto the curb? Yet this man, this lawyer, walked into my father's place of business that he created with his own two hands, and cut Gia and I out. He changed the course of my father's empire without him giving any consent to do it and he walks around free. Did he really think the will contest was going to be the end of all of this? Did he think that Gia and I were going to lay down and not put up a fight?

Well, I am still solo, and I am going to continue with my memoir and the right attitude, no matter what the circumstances. I had to find out why this stranger was still on the corporate paperwork of our family's business. I wondered off and on if he was extorting my family for financial reasons. I played offence/defense mental Olympics very well. If my family spoke up about what he did, he might threaten them and risk losing everything they had worked for, and he would keep them tied up in court for years bankrupting them. Therefore, I had to continue to lay low. Stay focused and keep chipping away at the story, but it felt like it was taking me forever to get to where I needed to go. It all seemed so overwhelming but again, I did have help and guidance from the universe.

The brother yorkie was never the same after his sister crossed the rainbow bridge. He would mope around the house with his sad puppy dog eyes. He would not get out of the dog stroller. He always walked with me. I used to call him my little Bruce Jenner because he could walk for hours and never want to take a break.

He refused to go outside on a walk unless I put him in the pet stroller because that is what his 'Sissy' did.

Growing frustrated, I decided to change up the routine. I thought we could take a road trip and that might distract us both a little bit, so we set off on an adventure.

Take an adventure I said to myself. I jumped in my pink race car "The Dodge" and we set off. My cars were meant to be driven on the highway anyway. Why have a high-performance car unless you're going to use it - open it up for a few hours on the highway.

I was supposed to go to Frenchy's Lake house first, but the plans fell through. Next try was the next friend and their lake house over the Labor Day weekend, it was hard to make plans or travel at that time. So, when those plans fell through, I asked a pen pal who lived in Scranton, Pennsylvania if she wanted a visitor.

It was a four hour drive each way. I figured leave in the morning and come back the next day. I made it in three and a half hours with one stop for coffee and gas. I had a blast. It was a fun day. We went shopping, and then out for a nice Italian dinner. I checked into the Holiday Inn Express. The next day my friend the country chick and I went to a crystal shop in town. She knew that was right up my alley. On the way there the engine seized. Driving down a winding road in the middle of a cornfield, the dashboard lit up like a Christmas tree and rump, rump, rump, dead. There was no cell signal for emergency roadside. The back end of my car was still on the road, front end partly on the shoulder. How was I going to move this car out of the way? I saw this in a movie once, so I always wear a dress on a road trip. Men recognize you faster in a dress. I had my hazards on, then I popped the hood, and leaned against the side of the car. Thank God I had that long multicolor sun dress on. After we sat there for forty-five minutes my guardian angels sent a gentleman to help. He helped push the car across the road where I suddenly had cell service! So, if that ever happens again, I will know to walk across the street to check for a cell signal. I called roadside assistance. My insurance company sent a flatbed tow. Off to the mechanic we went. Two days prior of my trip I had the oil changed, tires rotated, and a new battery installed. I thought let us work backwards since they just inspected it and gave me the green light for a road trip. Finally, after about three hours, we got to Firestone. They told us, "We will look at it and we will let you know."

I went to the waiting room, checked my cellphone battery, and started sending texts to my soul tribe back home. Now I was getting nervous because it looked like an expensive issue when the entire dash goes out and your engine stops. After about an hour of trying to walk Cupid back and forth, up and down the street, we returned to the front counter to find out the status. The woman said, "This vehicle needs to be towed to a Dodge dealership. We will not be able to get parts here for weeks. The dealership should have these parts in stock."

They checked over everything and determined it had nothing to do with a battery, oil, or fluid levels. So back to square one. Second time calling for roadside assistance that day. Next up was a tow to dealership. I was lucky there was a dealership close by. I got there fifteen minutes before closing. They checked me in and marked my paperwork ASAP.

The country chick called her brother, and he came and picked all of us up. It was a blessing I got a ride to the hotel and to the local

Walmart to buy dog food. The country girl looked something up on her Android and said to me. "The engine failure on your car is covered under the warranty. Dodge issued a timing gauge and timing chain safety bulletin which is synonymous with a safety recall. "A safety bulletin is the same thing as a safety recall, they renamed it that to release liability for putting faulty parts into your car."

They did send me a recall notice at 24,000 miles that the chain was defective and to have it replaced, so I did have it replaced at my local dealership.

I remember when I was driving with Sunshine, she mentioned that she heard a ticking noise under the hood and asked me why my engine did that. I explained to her that ever since I had the recall done that is the way the engine sounded.

The next morning, I was told the engine had a hole in the manifold, cam needed work, bent pistons, and the timing gauge broke that in turn broke the timing chain throwing engine out of time causing the pistons to be smacked around and so on. This is a common issue with these cars. There was a safety bulletin on this part five years back. If I would have waited and not had the service done when the recall came out, it would have been covered under warranty. I was told the cost to fix it would be $2900 in parts and labor. They would order parts and that it would take a day. Next day country gal did take me to Walmart again, dog food, snacks, bath bomb, wine.

Next morning no luck with the dealership getting parts in. Now I am missing work opportunities. No computer, only my phone. I stayed in bed the following day and called friends and asked their advice. I was stuck out in the country, I had no place to go, and I needed HELP fast. And now I was paying nightly for a hotel room, buying take-out food and other necessities, but still no information about the car. I start doing my own research. The timing gauge and the timing chain contained plastic parts. Whoever thought it would be okay to put a plastic part in a HEMI engine? We need to have a discussion. I understood that man made plastic in a form that could withstand the heat, but from how it was explained to me was that if they made the timing gauge metal then the chain and the gauge would rub up against each other, metal on metal. They made the gauge out of different materials and the plastic seemed to be what they figured would work. My issue was that my timing chain was not 100% metal, so it melted. That is why I had the customer safety bulletin performed. And that one failed me too. My car went approximately 45,000 miles on it with the new chain and then, it broke.

I told the dealership I wanted the car towed back home. I no longer wanted to wait around in a hotel room for parts to be delivered. I need to get home; I told them I would take the car to my mechanic's shop. They told me not to do that because I would have to pay one thousand dollars for towing, and according to them, this work would be covered under Dodge warranty.

I told the service manager that I decided to tow it home and could he please have someone pick me up at the hotel and take me to the dealership. I would have it towed home from there, He said that he would send someone and never did. Next day. I start making calls. Dodge would not cover the cost of the parts because I already had the work performed under the safety bulletin and those parts were only warrantied for two years.

I asked if those terms were stated anywhere? It did not say anywhere on the paperwork for the recall, in the bulletin, or on the website that there was any parts expiration date whatsoever.

I argued," if it is a recall, it is a recall. That is, it. Once you claim there is a problem, you take accountability for that, you always must until the issue is permanently remedied. Clearly it is not resolved because the problem still exists, why are you making your problems my problems? Your installing defective parts into my engine."

Three of us on a recorded line holding a conference call, Dodge corporate, the Service Manager, and myself. Once I told her what I knew to be true, click she disconnected the call and Dodge literally Dodged the issue. He said he would call me the next day and let me know if he was going to be able to fix this.

That night I turned to my spirituality. I called the Communicators they are a panel of psychics and mediums on the international BlogTalkRadio. Linda told me to rent a car and drive home the next day and let them fix the car if they agree to do so locally.

I went outside and it was pitch dark. I asked God to show me a sign that I was being protected by the heavens. I saw a little bench and I sat down. I looked up into the night sky and I kid you not, there it was. A bright yellow cross that was about six foot high illuminated in the sky from the church across the parking lot. I asked for a sign, and I received it.

Next day came. They said that they still won't have the parts for days but not to worry they would be able to get the parts and fix the car for me under warranty.

Labor Day weekend started on Friday, and I could not be stuck here all that time with no car and paying the nightly hotel rates, so, I rented a car and drove home. Thank goodness I had a credit card on me. Rental car companies do not use debit cards.

I needed to go to the dealership to get my apartment keys. The rental car place was across the street from the dealership. I asked the country chick if she would drive me to the dealership, and she said no. People are so disappointing. It was 11am and check out time. Cupid and I were sitting on a bench in front of the hotel and waiting for a rental car. Luck was with me. Enterprise came to me. I drove all this way to visit a friend for a change of scenery because when I looked out my apartment window all I saw was the parking lot and car license plates, and I will be damned if I was going to do the same thing hundreds of miles away. So, no matter where you roam, there you are. I was sitting there staring at a parking lot and car license plates. FML I thought!

As soon as I disconnected myself from that broken energy, my luck turned around. We jumped into a small Ford Focus and got on the road. It only cost $10 in gas, and we were home in four hours.

I ran and grabbed my wallet and put every credit card I had in it. Never again leaving the house with only one. That really could have been a crisis.

I did look at it like taking a vacation away from home to clear my head. I spent some money to get out of Dodge (no pun intended).

It worked. I was never so grateful for all the things I have in my life as I was the day I walked in that door. I said God, "never again will I complain about my life. It was perfect mess."

# Chapter Thirteen

A little fun fact about the "Cherry Bomb" (as I called her). She is one of the 245 that released into the United States in October of 2010, the other 255 remaining released into Canada. According to Road & Track, she is a "street-legal race car." She is a classic car, a special edition and a collector's item.

"Barbie Jet," "Cherry Bomb", Hemi engine, V-8 clean as a whistle. Complete with every maintenance record. Every time I drove her anywhere, people would pull out their camera phones and snap, snap, snap, away. I always took exceptionally loving care of her.

In 1973 the year I was born. Dodge came out with a Lollypop Pink Charger. Fast forward forty years, they produced a throwback. They called it the Furious Fuchsia Challenger. I was working at my family's company when it came out. I won the car in the sales competition. I sold $1 million dollars' worth of product in one year. I could buy any car I wanted that was pink. It was a match made in heaven.

Dealing with all that was happening with the "Cherry Bomb," my father has reincarnated within me. I loved it. I finally got it. Stand your own ground. Know your rights and know when your right. And if you can, hire a good lawyer.

The safety recall was issued on my car in 2014 on the timing gauge and chain. Failure of this part would cause severe engine failure. The engine would seize (as mine did) while driving. This was what the customer safety bulletin read.

Is a service bulletin the same as a recall?

What's The Difference Between a TSB and a Recall? Sometimes a TSB is confused with a recall. The main difference is that a recall is issued by a vehicle manufacturer for issues that are safety-related, while a TSB covers components that may be malfunctioning but don't compromise the safety of the vehicle.

If an engine failing is not a safety concern that compromises the vehicle's safety, then what is?

The next morning, I called and told the service manager that the car had a safety recall on it and all repairs are covered under warranty. They refused to honor it.

I called Fiat Chrysler Auto LLC and emailed the CEO but received nothing but the answer "NO." They put faulty parts in their cars so you can pay more to have the vehicle repaired later. I was not having it. The way I see it, the dealership makes money off you in two ways. First, when you purchase the vehicle and second when you have it serviced. The service department can write up service under warranty but if they do that and the manufacture does not cover the charges, the dealership will be held accountable, and it will also hurt their bottom line at the end of the year.

So, the original cost of the vehicle was obviously not too bad, but it cost 1/3 of the car's original purchase price to fix it to be able to drive it, when the engine failed at 65,000 miles. They have you at their mercy, even if you maintain your car properly. Even with my clean maintenance records, I was set up for failure by the same company who sold me the original product.

You can call class action lawyers, but once they get a huge settlement their phone lines become disconnected. One small person is not going to compete against the big three.

Of course, I did contact everyone. The BBB could not do anything because the manufacturer was operating in bankruptcy. I contacted the NHTSA, class action lawyers, the attorney general's office for both states, but came up duces.

I pointed out and emailed the link on their website that stated "FCA LLC" (Fiat Chrysler Automobiles) Safety Recalls are covered even if you are out of warranty, at no cost to you."

I had all the proof I needed for them to cover the cost by the manufacture, and they put me on mute.

I was frustrated so I took a walk to Target. I walked around pacing back and forth just to release all my anxiety and suddenly, I saw it down the last isle in the back of the store.

A black Huffy bike. I jumped on her and rode her around the store. After inquiring about the price, I applied for a Target credit card, received 10% off, and rode her back home. I parked the bike in my living room and immediately had to add a pet basket.

After installing the basket and putting Cupid inside, I padded him inside the basket with a pillow and a blanket, strapped him down, and off we went for a ride. I walked it all the way down the street to the park that had a walking path. I figured it was a paved path and that would be good practice for me. It was much harder to balance the bike with Cupid moving around in the basket than I expected. I rode for a few laps and started back home. I guess I started getting cocky because I had mastered that smooth, paved path, so I jumped onto the sidewalk. I came down on the handlebars, and I nearly face planted on the curb but luckily, I was able to control the bike enough to jump off and steady it.

I start walking down the street back home when I heard, "Mam, Mam are you okay?"

I looked over my shoulder and I see a man walking towards me from behind. First thing I could smell was his cologne and it was heavenly.

I said, "Yea I am."

"Then why are you walking your bike with your dog in it and not riding it." He chuckled to me.

I immediately knew he was a wise guy and started laughing myself. I told him the story about how I just purchased the bike and it's been a minute since I have ridden on one. He told me that when I brought the bike home, I should have adjusted it to my height, and then tightened the handlebars with an Alan wrench to be safe.

I said "I would have never of thought of that, but judging from what happened, I guess you would be correct. They assembled it but I had to adjust it to my height. Yes, that makes perfect sense."

He asked me where I lived, and I pointed straight ahead and said, "Right there in those apartments." He told me that he lived there too. We where neighbors.

He also mentioned that he was a Marine. He followed me home. After I retrieved the Alan wrench, we walked to the nearby picnic area and started talking as he tightens the bolts on my bike. I told him the whole story about the Dodge breakdown and asked him if he would go with me down there to get my car back. He not only fixed my bike but agreed to help me retrieve my car! Once again, the universe sent me a guardian angel.

Now, let me tell you about the Marine. He was approximately 6'2", solid muscular build with legs like tree trunks. I doubt he had over 4% body fat. I imagined angel wings on him and instantly felt extremely safe in his presence. The next day I was going back and forth once again with the dealership. Now that I had muscle behind me, I was confident I would get my car back this time, but I did not. Now, it had been two weeks. They gave me no information on my car for two solid weeks. I finally decided to send a tow truck.

I received a phone call from the tow truck driver. I knew it was going to cost me $1,000.00 to have the car towed back home, but

he was calling to inform me that the dealership would not release
the car to him until the bill was paid.

"What bill needs to be paid?" I asked.

"The service manager said you have a $3,202.09 invoice that is
due," he replied.

"No, I should not have any charges at all! Just let me call there and
I will call you back."

I hung up and called the service manager. The service manager told
me that he had ordered the parts for my car and even though the
car was still not running I still had to pay for parts and labor, or
they were going to file a mechanics lien on it and start charging me
for storage at the rate of $250.00 per day.

My car did not run, and I never signed off on any paperwork giving
them authority to charge me anything. I must pay a tow truck
driver $1,000, and $3202.09 for repairs that were never done. I had
sent emails and asked for updates and nothing for two solid weeks.
Nothing until I said I was sending a tow truck.

I was being extorted. I started feeling like they wanted to keep this
car for themselves and were doing anything and everything they
could to keep me from getting it back! They would sink the owner
with storage fees and make it nearly impossible for them to get
their car out of hock and then sell it to the next person that came

by or in my case, since it was such a classic, keep it for themselves and add to their car collection.

I called a friend whose husband is an attorney and he walked me though the entire process about how to get my car back. I called the local police in the town where the car dealership was. The police officer there told me to come there with my proof of ownership and they would have the car released to me.

The local police told me to call the county sheriff's office. I explained to the sheriff's office that the dealership had no authorization to work on my car and that I was told the parts were covered under warranty but when Dodge said they were not going to pay for the repairs I told the dealership that I wanted to have it towed to my local mechanic and they were now refusing to release the car to the tow truck driver. If they had fixed the car, I would be more than happy to pay the bill, but the reality was that they had this car for over two weeks and did nothing but charge me $3202.09. The manager of the service department said that I had given a verbal authorization to work on the car. I gave them permission to look at my car to diagnose the problem. When they said the parts and labor were covered under warranty, I was all for them completing the job. But at no time after being told Dodge would not cover the cost under warranty, did I give a dealership authorization to do any work. I never signed off on anything! The sheriff told me that the dealership could enact a Mechanical Lien because they replaced parts on the car. I told the officer that if the mechanic worked on my car and if indeed, they replaced parts on my car, it would be running. But my car did not run and so I could not drive it home, nothing was fixed. I explained to the officer that

I would soon be on my way down there to retrieve the car myself and tow it back.

I called the Marine and told him what was going on. He told me to get him, and he would go down there with me to get my car back. Enterprise rented me an SUV capable of towing a car transporter and we were on our way.

I called the sheriff to let him know when we were in range. They met us at the dealership. Arriving at the dealership, I spoke to the officers first and again explained the situation.

The officer stated, "This dealership repairs all our police vehicles, and we are not going to allow your car to be released until your bill is paid."

I was angry, "This is a legal matter, and you cannot play judge here! This is a contract dispute that can be litigated in Federal Court. I am across state lines. A police officer is to keep the peace, not play judge, jury and executioner. Is your body camera on?" I asked.

He replied, "It is on."

That moment is when I learned when Obama was president, he bailed out Chrysler and General Motors. Many government contracts made Dodge Chargers their official municipal vehicle. Knowing this, the police took the dealership's side. I was out muscled. I mean I could see their side. Chrysler had government contracts, so they rely on that to cover their bottom line. They sold these special edition cars to the collectors and then they nickeled and dimed the bottom feeder consumer.

I paid the bill since I had no other choice if I wanted to get my muscle car back. The service manager told me I had to pay with Cash, Certified Check, Money Order, or debit card. That was so I could not dispute the charge. After I paid for the car, I asked to see it. They took us down to the second level and the Cherry Bomb was pushed all the way back into the corner covered in dust, they had her in storage.

They said, "We will push your car outside, but you have twenty-four hours to get it off the lot before we start charging storage fees."

I explained to them that I would be back after I rented the towing equipment from U-Haul. They pushed the car all the way out, but into a very tight corner of the parking lot that had a long twisting driveway that went from the underground storage area of the dealership to the above ground where the showroom was located. They purposely stuck it way back in the corner to make it even harder for us to tow it out of the lot. They were prepared. I was not.

I showed up at the local U-Haul place at five minutes to five. They had no record of my online reservation and no equipment there for me to rent. There was no equipment at all within a 100-mile radius of our location.

At that point, the Marine took his shirt off and the tattoo that went from shoulder to shoulder across his muscular chest had the inscription, "My brother's keeper" with angel wings on each side. I knew it. I knew it when I met him on that sidewalk that day that the universe sent me an angel.

He said "Let's drive back home, rent the equipment there, and come back down here tomorrow. "The clock is ticking let's go." With those words, we set back for the long road trip home.

# Chapter Fourteen--------

I had to return the rental car and start the process all over from scratch. It was a bright sunny morning, and the Marine was up and ready as usual to pull the trigger and be my soldier. I called a local U-Haul store. Oleg had the best reviews in the neighborhood. We were in luck; he had an auto transport hitch available.

Next up was the rental car company. The Marine told me to make sure that I was able to tow a vehicle with the pickup truck (which I had no knowledge of how that worked as I was a newbie at this kind of stuff.) I told the rental car person that I needed a pickup truck. I did not go into details about what I would be towing.

They rented me a minivan. I drove back over to the U-Haul place, and the Marine looked at me with a shocked expression on his face. He looked scared and confused at the same time.

"What is this? We are not planning a family vacation, I said to get a tow vehicle!"

"I said I needed a heavy-duty vehicle, and they rented me this," I replied.

Oleg came out of the U-Haul office and said, "That will not tow a car. You must go back and tell them you need a pickup truck."

Now I was confused, so I sighed and returned to the rental car office. Lucky for me the lady who was waiting on me was uber patient. I explained that I was picking up a piece of machinery and I needed something more heavy duty. She understood and called the dealership down the street that she had an agreement with. She told me they were going to rent me a truck for the day, but I needed to have it back by 8am the next morning. It was a special request, and she was more than willing to help me out, but it was indeed a special favor. I agreed to have it returned by 8am.

A man pulled up in a Dodge Ram double cab truck with towing capabilities and I climbed inside the truck and drove back to Oleg's office.

I was met with big smiles on both men's faces. Oleg was a good man. He took his time hooking up the trailer to the truck and explained to us how to secure the car to the trailer and gave me specific instructions not to drive faster than 65 mph the entire time.

He said, "Girl, go get your car back. When you return the trailer just park it over there, I will not be here that early in the morning."

We piled into the pickup and started driving. The Marine told me to go slow. He wanted me to practice driving with an empty trailer on the back of the truck because there was no weight on the back end it was going to jump around especially when I turned corners.

I drove ten and two on the wheel. We decided to bring Cupid back home. It was going to be a long day and why make him nervous. I placed two bowls of food and water out and laid four pee pads on the kitchen floor and we took off.

I took the turn way to fast out of the apartment complex and almost lost the trailer within twenty feet of leaving my place.

The marine looked at me and said, "GO SLOW! No coffee for you!"

When we arrived at the dealership, they were already closed. It took some time for us to back the pickup truck with the trailer down the winding lower-level driveway to the back parking lot. Because the pickup was large, and the car was in the smallest part of the back corner, we wiggled our way down it and got it as close as possible.

We both got behind the car and pushed and pushed, but with no luck. We could not get it up the ramp. It was useless. We needed a winch. All the time Oleg spent with us, it never occurred to us that we would need this and of course it was late and none of the stores were open. How were we going to get this car up on the carport? We both started to get very aggravated. We needed help and once again found ourselves in a pickle.

"Look it has been a long two days. Let us get something to eat and we can figure it out after. Nothing good comes when you are thinking at the same time as being hangry!" I said.

He replied, "I am going to drive this time."

I hoisted myself up into the passenger seat and we drove around the town. Nothing was open. I pulled out my cellphone and opened the Google map app. I typed, food near me. Score! There was a twenty-four-hour hamburger shop open for drive thru orders only. We drove over to the restaurant and looked at the menu.

"I will take a chicken sandwich and a medium French fries extra ketchup." I yelled over the Marine and into the drive thru speaker.

"I will take three double cheeseburgers and a large Coca-Cola." He spoke into the speaker.

I paid for our meals, and we parked nearby in an empty parking lot.

We felt so defeated. I ate my sandwich and left the fries in the bag. I decided to jump out of the truck and relieved myself over in a patch of bushes that was off to the side.

The marine never looked at me while I was peeing on the side of the road but after I returned to the truck, he decided to take his turn. We both looked at each other and started laughing.

I told him to take the food and throw it out in the trash bin. He said, "I think we will keep your fries; I may get hungry later."

I replied, "The left-over food is going to smell up the truck and I'd rather not smell this to be honest, let's dump it now while we can."

He very sternly replied, "You must have grown up rich. In my house we never threw anything good out, so I am going to keep it for later."

I rolled my eyes and looked out the passenger side window as he drove back to the dealership. We sat there thinking of how we could get this car up on the car transport.

I suddenly had it. "I know what to do! Why not call roadside assistance and have them pull the car up onto the car transport. Technically the car does not run, and I do have roadside assistance."

He said "That may work. Even if they can tow it up to the second level, we would not be struggling to push it up this hill."

He pulled the truck and the trailer into the parking lot, and I started dialing roadside assistance.
We were on the phone with roadside assistance for what seemed like hours, only to find out that of course, there was only one person within a 50-mile radius of our location that was on their list. The man named Gary, said that he would not come and tow a vehicle out of a dealership at midnight.

I told Gary that we could have the police come there because I have my title and the local police are very aware of who I was and why I was there trying to tow this car. But I guess Gary's wife would not see it that way and hung up the phone on me. The operator for Geico roadside assistance said there was nothing that she could do and eventually stopped answering my phone calls. We were out of luck.

I told the Marine to pull the truck in front of the driveway to the dealership blocking the service entrance and that we would have to wait until the morning for them to help us. After all, they put us in this position, and they did everything they could to prevent us from retrieving my car so now we are going to block them.

I decided to sleep in the back cab, and he took the front seat. The bright lights of the dealership peered in through the windshield, and I wondered how we were going to get any sleep.

I took my Chanel Covid19 facemask and pulled it over my eyes and I quickly started counting sheep. I awakened to a women's voice screaming outside. I quickly reached into my purse and grabbed my switchblade.

"Michael where are you?"

"Michael where are you?"

"Michael I am here where are you?"

The voice was close. I felt as if I could almost hear her breathing. All I could think of was those darn French fries. This person was walking through the parking lot and must have smelled the left-over food I told the Marine to throw away!

He whispered, "Stay down, stay low, whatever you do, you cannot make a sound."

I saw a woman's hand touch the side of the truck and then I heard footsteps running away and she moved on.
The marine said, "It had to be someone who was coming down

from a drug high and she was a straggler."

"I told you to throw those fries away. People are animals no different than any other mammal and no doubt she was hungry looking for food." I scolded him.

He turned his body around and went back to sleep. Three hours later I opened my eyes, and the Marine was already up watching employees showing up for work.

The first man to approach the truck was a semi-truck driver. He walked up to the driver's side window and motioned to the Marine to roll his window down. The Marine complied and the driver asked him if he was there to make a delivery. The Marine told him no, he was waiting for the dealership to open so roadside assistance would be able to come and tow our car out of the bottom back lot. The semi driver walked back to his truck and the Marine rolled his window back up.

As we anxiously waited for the dealership to open at 9 am, we saw one person after another walk past our truck, never asking us why we had the truck blocking the service entrance. Nobody asked us if we needed help, nada, nothing just dead silence as we were ignored by all the workers who walked by showing up for their shift.

Finally, at 8:45 am two men walked up to the truck and the Marine rolled the window down. "Excuse me sir, we need to ask you to move your truck. It is blocking the service entrance."

I replied, "We will move the truck once you help us get my car out of the hole you put it in down the ramp and load it up on our trailer. We have been here all night and slept in this truck and we are not leaving here without my car."

The two men looked at each other and the one said to the other, "Get the power pusher and let's get her car loaded ASAP."

And just like that all the blocks where released. They knew that I was serious, and I was intent on interrupting their business until they finished helping me with mine.

Two men from the dealership turned into three and the Marine. They pushed that car all the way up the driveway and then they pushed it up onto the car transport. The Marine did exactly what Oleg said to do with all the cables and after securing the Dodge, we finally left. I drove two seconds down the street and spotted an open McDonald's. I drove around and bypassed the drive thru. I took up a few spots in the back of the lot and looked at the Marine as I parked the truck.

I pulled my purse into the front seat and pulled out a clear cellophane wrapped package of sweetgrass. "We need to burn this all around the car and inside of it. I am not driving one more minute down the road until we smudge this entire car as well as ourselves of any negativity."

He did not blink an eye at my suggestion. He took the package from my hands, and I handed him a lighter. We took turns smudging ourselves and then he jumped up on top of the car transport opened the driver's side door and smudged the entire inside of the Cherry bomb. His legs where so strong and you could see every muscle outlined as he wore super short shorts. I had never seen muscles like his on anyone. He had the body of a professional athlete. I do remember him saying he was fresh out of the reserves. One could tell his body had been trained in a way one could only get from serving our country. There was not one ounce of fat on his entire physique. He walked all around the car and did not question my line of thinking.

He jumped off the trailer and put the smoke out. I told him "Let's go inside and grab a quick breakfast and some coffee before we get on the road."

He replied, "I would just love to use a restroom."

As we walked inside, there leaning against the booth adjacent to the bathroom wall was the lady. The one who was yelling in the dealership parking lot at 3am. The only reason I knew it was her was because she very clearly was still strung out on drugs and kept mumbling the same words over and over. I quickly ran into the lady's restroom, relieved myself and ran up to the front counter. I ordered us breakfast sandwiches a coffee and an orange juice and returned to the truck.

"What happened? I looked around the restaurant, but you already left without me." the Marine said to me.

"I am sorry. Anxiety took over when I saw that lady slumped over the booth and I realized that no matter how bad you think you got it, someone is always worse off," I tearfully replied.

He took the orange juice and breakfast sandwiches out of my hands. Unwrapped one and handed it to me. "Drive slow just like I told you the entire way home. If you get tired and you want to stop, we will stop. If you need to stretch your legs, we will pull over, but at no time will you drive over 65 mph otherwise we are going to lose this entire load." He spoke those words as he stared directly into my eyes.

I took three deep breaths and started the drive back home. It was not a very entertaining ride back home. The Marine fell asleep about thirty minutes into the drive, and I watched the road. I used my cruise control and thought about the rental car lady and if she was going to ream me out for not complying with her terms, that truck was indeed not going to be back on time, and in fact, not even the same day. Nevertheless, I continued to concentrate on the drive.

I made it all the way home and safely dropped the Cherry Bomb off at the garage mechanic's home.

We went to Oleg's office, and he asked us how the trip went. I said, "They did everything they could to prevent me from getting my car back, but we did it and I thank you from the bottom of my heart for all your help."

Next stop was the rental car office. I was hesitant on going back there because I did not honor the agreement of returning the truck in the morning as I had promised. It really was out of my control. I prayed that the lady would be understanding towards me, and I could return it with no issues. I pride myself on standing by my word, but I really could not help breaking this promise.

I pulled up at the rent a car office and it was closed. I looked up and said, "Thank you good Lord for answering my prayers." I dropped the keys in the overnight box and drove off feeling relieved.

The mechanic called me and told me that the hole in the manifold had been caused by the dealership. He said that they also broke an electrical component in my car. The only thing they did the entire time they had my car was caused more damage. He said he was going to have to take the entire top block off the engine and completely rebuild it. The pistons were bent, and he wanted to take his time taking my engine apart. He emailed me a second recall that was issued to mechanics only. He belonged to a computer system that mechanics use to look up parts and dealer recalls. Dodge did issue a second recall on those parts eighteen months ago. He said that the first problem I had was I paid for parts and repairs that never happened at the dealership, and the second problem was that I should be reimbursed from Dodge because the second recall on those parts had been issued and he emailed me the proof.

When I first got the car, I joined the Challenger Forums online. There were a couple of them. Challenger Talk was the one I was most active on. I scoured the posts but could not find anything about the second recall or that customers were ever notified about it including myself. It was only issued to the mechanics, which was very shady on Mopar's part.

Since I did not see anything, I decided to post a thread about it myself. People told me to use the @dodgecares in the posts and see if they would respond. So, that is what I did. I posted the photo of my car on the car transport, in front of the dealership showing the name of it and stated my claim. I heard nothing back. I spent days and weeks researching the issue and I was able to find information online from a Dodge employee who worked in the Detroit plant. What he stated was that the correct parts for the timing chain were not available until the late fall of 2016. So, the recall that I had in

2014 replacing the defective parts with more defective parts went from being a safety recall to a "Stella Problem".

I notified Dodge corporate about the extortion from their dealership, and I did dispute the charge on my bank debit card, but I got nowhere. Whenever possible, pay by credit card. Anytime you try to dispute something with a debit card even with all the proof that I had, the banks will not reverse the charge. The credit card companies have more power when it comes to disputes verses banks. I submitted a written statement from my mechanic and everything. The mechanic stated that the service department caused more damage to my engine and never installed any new parts although they did charge me for them.

Nothing and I mean nothing returned any of the money back to me that I spent out of pocket.

Since the actual full metal recall parts were not available until 2016. The original recall that was done on my Challenger two years prior in 2014 did nothing for us car owners but released Mopar from their liability of the problem. How many people did this effect? I was not the only one.

I searched for other victims who got the run around like I did, but most of the people either did not speak up or did not like the fact I was speaking up for others who could not speak for themselves. Mopar was dodging the issue. Ultimately, I ended up having to take out a $10,000.00 loan to pay for all of this. All money was out of my pocket and of course I never heard back from Dodge even after I mailed them all the receipts with a letter that said, "YOU OWE ME $8K." Does Dodge Care? It cost me 1/3 of the original purchase price of the car. Never again. I am a Chevy Girl for life!

# Chapter Fifteen

I decided to go back down to Florida but this time I picked the east side and flew into Boca Raton. It was the first weekend Boca Raton was open. Mizner Park is the Beverly Hills of Southwest Florida and there was a home in town I was looking to purchase.

Florida was pretty much wide open, even with Covid and it felt so freeing to be able to go to the ocean once again. I made friends with a girl down there who was the girlfriend of a man I had developed a friendship with from my finance company. I had a tough time finding a VRBO and it would have been hard to stay in the Hotel with Cupid, plus rent a car. I wanted the local experience. She asked me if I wanted to stay at her place for a couple of days since she lived so close to Boca.

After all the work I had done on my case, and all the time I spent attempting to expose corruption, I found I had become paranoid about everything. I was always afraid that someone was going to rob me that whenever I traveled, I brought whatever cash I had, and my most valuable possessions with me. So, there I was with everything I owned with me just in case someone robbed my apartment back home, and who did I end up spending my time in Florida with? A thief.

As it turned out, my new friend was a Kleptomaniac. Kleptomaniacs steal because they want to see how much they can get away with. They steal things in plain sight, and they are particularly good at it.

She started stealing from me slowly. Shortly after she picked me up at the airport, I could not find my lighter.

Red flag number one. My lighter was the first item she lifted.

Red flag number two was after our trip to Target when I could not find my Chanel facemask that was in my purse.

Red flag number three was after my trip to the pool.

She said she would watch my Yorkie while I was at the pool, so I asked her to order some food for lunch. Now keep in mind that because I was staying at her apartment while in Florida, I brought her a Victoria Secret gift basket, so I considered myself a great houseguest. All that did was let her see where my weakness was. I was kind to her and that was my weakness. While I was at the pool, she made her way through my things. When I got back, I grabbed my wallet to pay for the food and noticed it was a bit lighter than before I left.

I knew right then and there she stole cash out of my wallet. What a dummy I was leaving my purse behind while I was at the pool. She helped herself to $200.00, which by the way, is the most that you can steal that is a misdemeanor. I was leaving the next morning. but I had to report it to the police.

The police officer I reported the theft to asked, "How do you know this person?"

"She is the girlfriend of a guy I know from my Finance Company. I could not rent a house because of Covid19, and I have my dog with me, so she said I could stay with her for a couple of days. When I went to the pool, she went through my things. She stole $200 cash, my lighter, and my Chanel facemask. I found out she had been ordering on my Uber Eats account for days. She must have taken photos of my debit cards because when I figured out what was going on, I deleted my credit cards off the app."

He said "Then you need to cut the ties with her boyfriend too. Pay attention to who your friends are. Birds of a feather flock together."

I showed him the proof of the order notification that I did not place. She had done it four times, using my credit card information. Shame on me, I was the dummy that left my wallet and things behind.

I worked with Uber Eats to get her IP address blocked so she could not order from there again. I cancelled all my credit cards, put a fraud alert on my bank accounts, and blocked everyone on Facebook associated with her bad energy.

I have always referred to Florida as the land of the convicted felons. The whole state's system is designed to fit the criminal on the lam. I have been down there many times and I have never felt any different. Vacation there, sure but when you do, bring disposable everything. Leave it all there.

I say learn to trust the journey. Everything comes at a price. Stay in a reputable place, take care of your business. Enjoy the scenery along the way. Those walls your staring at will be there when you get home, and like Dorothy said, "there is no place like home."

# Chapter Sixteen

The email read," Hi, I hope you are well. Against my better judgement, I held onto your Ms.Pac-Man machine, and it was not right. I was advised to do it, but I was not thinking clearly. I am sorry for that. The machine has always been in the garage and was never touched. Please let me know when you want to get it and I will make sure it is ready for your pickup. Gia"

I responded back that I would be there later today, and she replied, "I will have it outside after 2:30pm."

So, I called one of my friends and asked if they thought it, was a trap.

My friend replied, "Well go get her! Your dad bought you that game back in what year?"

"I think it was 1999," I replied.

"Well, the universe is giving you your arcade game back so get a truck and retrieve it but bring someone with you!"

I contacted my neighbor, the Marine and he said he would go with me. We showed up at Oleg's office once again. We rented a van and we set off on our journey.

He pulled over to a coffee shop and jumped out. "I will be right back."

I felt so fortunate in that moment. I sat there with an abundance of gratitude. The universe had me covered even if at short notice. I thought to myself, "This is why I can offer forgiveness." I spent so much time hating on Koger that I lost track of who I was. I was still spying on him. There should never be an argument when you present the facts. I included all the evidence in my case, in my memoir 'Shattered Windows'. The reality was that I called Koger out for forgery. Forgery has no expiration date. You can always be charged with forgery. I alleged that he was extorting money from my siblings. Nobody should have been paying this guy anything. He comes in, makes a mess of my father's legacy, and then charges them, for the difference. When Koger showed up on the scene, Gia and I got our throats slit and he still is walking around free. Never mind the reality that we worked like workaholics in that business. No one had time for a personal life. When you are running a family business, all of you are constantly aligned and should always move forward united.

So, I am calling his bluff. He knows I'm still watching him. Like I always say, "Karma never forgets an address." For the rest of that man's life, he must live with what he did. I will fully heal when justice is served. To me, this would be the best thing that ever happened to our family; finding that one lawyer who is going to step up and call this guy out. Nobody has all the power all the time. Potentially, he could be the downfall of his entire law firm. Koger has entitlement issues, but he is great at his job. By now his law firm has grown exponentially. The man's got the skills to pay the bills, I must give that to him.

The door opened and the Marine handed me a black coffee, creamer and Stevia and got in his seat. Then he reached into a small bag and pulled out a strawberry sprinkled donut.

"Eat this, the calories do not matter. I know you avoid sugar, but we are going to work it off today. Enjoy life a little, go ahead, you can have it." That was the best donut I have ever eaten in my life.

The Marine asked, "Did you find out where it's at?"

"The email says it's in the garage, so let's go to her house."

At this point it had been over three- and one-half years since I had seen either the Ms.Pac-Man machine or my sister Gia. I originally dropped it off at her building, but wouldn't she have said it was still there in the email?

At two thirty in the afternoon, we arrived at Gia's house, but there was nothing sitting outside. So, we put on our masks, left the Yorkie in the van, and walked up the sidewalk to the front door. I had my Marine assistant there to run interference for me.

The house looked so different then when I walked out three years before. The landscaping changed, old plantings had been pulled up and hauled away. Like the plants, Gia had put down new roots. I bet that made her family feel energized. Christmas lights adorned the front and side yards. It looked like the children were enjoying the holidays. Staying home during the pandemic made everyone grateful to have a roof over their heads. Stepping up to the front door, the old system with cameras everywhere had been replaced with a simple ring doorbell. We rang the bell.

I heard, "I have to call you back; my sister is at my front door." Gia opened the door, and her dog ran out and latched onto my leg with such force it was like he never wanted to let me go.

"I am here to pick up the game, but I don't see it out here."

She replied, "It's outside at my store."

As we turned around to walk off the front steps, the dog would not let my leg go. I tried to gently pull him off me, but to no avail.

Gia yelled out to the Marine, "Could you?" He picked up the dog and brought him back up to the door. The door shut swiftly behind us.

Three years had gone by and that was all she had to say. Well OK then.

We put the address of the store into the GPS and were on to the next stop.

About fifteen minutes later we pulled into the dark parking lot and there she was, sitting outside in the cold with a thin grey blanket over her. Leaning on her right side was a large pink accent mirror, a picture of Santa and a vase with a red head on it that used to sit on my kitchen counter. "Julia" I called her.

I said to the Marine "Well the good news is, I got my stuff back, some of it anyway. Looks like Santa was here to show us that the spirit of Christmas is to Believe. She really did not have to store my things at all. I am sure the universe was just safely protecting these things until it was safe for me to have them again."

I was trying not to go into attack mode and be angry, blaming her for everything. This time I would put my big girl panties on and be grateful, for whatever reason she returned everything to me. But, as I looked around at my things sitting on the curb, the old feelings of abandonment crept back in. Just like what she did to me at her house, she threw everything, including me out on the curb with no remorse for her actions. She had the opportunity to talk to me and she turned her back on me once again.

I consider my relationship with Gia to be like a full-blown divorce. Not only did that ship sail, but it also sank. I can honestly say that Gia broke my heart. But I am also not the sister she knew anymore. I stand on my own two feet now, and nobody is going to put me down anymore.

But remembering Gia, it did not matter where we went together, we were a mighty energy duo. One day Gia came to my house and said, "Let's go to lunch." We went to a fancy seafood restaurant a few towns over. We walked in and sat at the bar and thought nobody else, but the bartender was there. We ordered two drinks and looked the lunch menu. The bartender came up to us and said, "The man sitting over there bought your drinks."

So, we both looked over our shoulders and waved him a thank you.

About five minutes went by and the bartender walked back by and said, "The man who bought you the drinks wants to know if you would have lunch with him?"

So, I looked over at Gia and said, "Sure, why not." Gia looked at me like, really, why did you do that? But it was no different than we had lunch with our dad. He was an older man, and we were not going to do anything. And I for one, was always grateful for a free meal. I got up from the bar, grabbed my purse and sat down. Gia followed soon after. We ordered lunch, were having a general conversation with him, and that was when he slumped over to one side and had a stroke.

We called over the bartender, who called 911 and the restaurant manager, moments later he was getting help. I grabbed my purse and motioned to Gia, "Let's go."

We started walking and we never looked back. We walked over to a Homegoods store where we spotted a hanging basket chair, made for two. We both looked at each other and ran over to sit in it and swing. As soon as we sat down, the chain broke, and we were on the ground rolling with laughter. I can still remember looking up at the sales associate as she was asking us if we were okay, but we could not answer her because we could not catch our breath long enough to stop laughing. When we did get up off the floor, Gia turned her head and said, "It's defective, send it back." And we got back in her Hummer and drove off.

There was a part of me that was happy Gia, and I did not reconcile because I knew I was going to move forward with my plan. It was better that I was the sacrificial lamb. After all, she did have two special needs children and it was better I took the bullets than her.

Suddenly, a garage door opened, and a man came running out.

"I am Jorge's brother, you need help?"

The Marine yelled back "Na man, we're good. We are loading these things up and we will be on our way soon."

The man looked like he had not showered in some time. I thought he might be living in the old building. He scurried off across the street to the liquor store. He later came wandering back with a six pack of beer. He reopened the garage door and went inside, rolling the door back down behind him. I thought to myself, "What is going on over here? What has Gia gotten herself into now?"

The Marine picked up the machine with both arms and carried it in like a bag of groceries. I almost fell over. We loaded up and left.

The next day came, and I still was trying to stop my old feelings of abandonment. I remembered Gia still had a set of keys belonging to my Chevy Monte Carlo – the one I called the "Bumble Bee", so I sent an email, "Thank you for keeping my arcade game in storage. It was never your obligation to do so. It's in perfect working condition. BTW, do you have the extra set of keys to my car?"

She responded, "Oh yes, they're here, still hanging on the wall. I will put them in the lower mailbox, and you can pick them up."

I emailed back, "I will be there on Friday."

I picked up the keys Friday night and for some reason everything pulled on my heart strings. Friday happened to be the day before my birthday.

The next email to Gia I will admit, was not the best of Stella. It said, "Contact me again, and I will contact the sheriff". Why I did that, I couldn't say but it was all I had left in me. I was left with that incredibly sad existence.

There would be a few more instances where Gia would use third party interference to send me messages, but in my mind it was over. I cannot and I will not ever return to the past or the person I once was. The siblings get no more of my time or energy. Nobody gets free rent inside my head.

# Chapter Seventeen

Frenchy called and told me that her father was in the hospital with Covid. For the time being I would have to give him time to recover to continue proofreading or find another editor. All I could do at that moment in time was to think back to my relationship with my father. I needed to be there for my friend. The book could wait. I put the memoir on the back burner and lent my support to my friend.

My father loved his family vacations. One summer, all eight of us flew to Disney World. By then, Jan was seriously dating a man and he accompanied because he was like family. Our last night at the Magic Kingdom, we watched the electric parade and afterward, walked the streets of Disney World. Instead of leaving with the rest of the crowd, we all hung out in front of Cinderella's castle and once all the chaos slowed down, we would leave.

We all left my parents sitting on a park bench and we all walked over to the fence. On the other side of the fence was a row of bushes that surrounded the castle. The castle was built up high. One by one we hoped the fence and ran up the lawn to the castle. A large wooden arch shaped door with black arrows on the hinges was so inviting. It was telling us to walk in. We all ran inside.

We all split up. Some took the service elevator or the stairs. Tina and I went exploring together. We opened one of the doors and started across the room. The table was set for the next breakfast that would be served at the castle. We started giggling and when we looked to the left, Mike the security guard was outside looking in at us through the glass. As fast as any of our legs could carry us, we all exited the castle and ran back to the bench. We all walked out of the park without any issues. We laughed about it for hours. It was such a good time and a memory I'll never forget.

Four months went by, the holidays were behind us, and my editor lost his battle with Covid. He was a retired English teacher who specialized in grammar. I needed time to regroup mentally. I once again sat down and started putting ad's out for a new editor. Lori answered my prayer. We worked perfect together. She was retired and didn't need to be paid immediately. She helped me improve my skills. The book came alive once again.

# Chapter Eighteen

I got up early one Sunday morning, drank my black coffee, let my dog out to go potty, and packed up the Monte Carlo to drive to the laundromat. I hated going to the laundromat. It sucked. Every time I had to go to the laundromat, I felt like a fish out of water.

Laundromats are usually open 24/7, and at any time of the day anything can walk through those doors. I would say most of the time people where there legitimately doing laundry, but the other 20% of the time it's where the "tarantulas" spend time together. I know they have attendants that clean the machines but putting my clothes in the machine after God only knows whose were in that machine prior to mine always made me cringe. Also, it's expensive - double the cost that was market rate. What choice did I have though? I always sat in my car, ran errands, or got a bite to eat, anything to stay outside while my clothes were washing and drying. That laundromat energy was so crazy that all I wanted to do was run back home.

They always had the television on and so loud you could barely hear yourself think. There was the young mom with the unruly kids who attempt to keep her kids in line as they waited for their laundry to be done. There were groups of laundromat coworkers who stood at the tables, folding endless piles of towels and families who would gather around a small table eating snacks out of the vending machines.

It was a three hour journey no matter how I looked at it and never at any time was it fun. The bonus at the laundromat vs my apartment complex was the dryers actually worked. The dryers never dried my clothes in one cycle at the apartment building because the maintenance guys never vacuumed out the lines, so it was double the money to attempt to dry my clothes.

That Sunday, after packing up all my laundry baskets and the detergent, I drove down the street to the laundromat and before I could get very far, the red brake light lit up on my dash and the car would not come to a stop. My brakes went out.

I finally rolled to a stop, popped open the hood and saw nothing. I called my garage mechanic who was currently working on the Dodge and asked him what I should do. He told me not to drive the car. I mean obviously but beyond that what should I expect?

He suggested that I buy brake fluid and see if that helped and if not to have the car towed to his shop. I said yes, I can do that, but now you have both of my cars, and I will have none. He assured me that my Dodge would be ready within the week.

I walked to the closest convenience store and bought two bottles of brake fluid. I was able to get back home after filling the reservoir with brake fluid but then the brake light went back on.

Suddenly, it occurred to me that I had just released a video trailer on YouTube about my book release. What if they cut my brake line? Was it to send a message of what was to come if I continued to speak the truth? Was it an attempt to scare me off?

Possibly, but this type of pain could not go unanswered. I unloaded the laundry and called the mechanic back to let him know the second car will be on its way for repairs shortly. After an inspection, the mechanic told me that my brake lines needed to be replaced.

I said "Really, what exactly needs to be replaced?"

"The front driver's side needs to be replaced." He responded.

I asked him "How often does something like that happen?"

He said, "Not too often – maybe 5%."

I did not ask him anything more and I just told him to replace the brake line. I was not going to elaborate on the bad company I had was associated with.

When you try explaining to people that you are a whistleblower against a corrupt law firm, you're usually riding solo. After that incident, I no longer drove with anyone as a passenger in any of my cars. So, the chances of someone cutting my brake line were 95%? Too coincidental for my peace of mind.

# Chapter Nineteen

In October I finished applying at all the literary agents I had found online. Over the course of 2020 I applied at approximately 2800 agencies. I knew the Coronavirus slowed everything down. At the same time, I was thinking if I could find an agency during the hard times, that would be a good sign.

I wanted to work as much as I could publishing my story.

After further research on my memoir, it appeared it was an open door for a lawsuit, so I consulted with a free lawyer who worked Pro Bono.

We had a phone call and an email exchange. I was very prepared and went straight to all the points. I took on the responsibility for publishing responsibly.

My first book was one giant ad for lawyers who are looking to take the time to correct an injustice. Koger, his law firm, the county and the city were also to blame for allowing this corruption in the court system. All these systems had failed me.

I was issuing a safety recall. I needed to be heard. I thought that once the book was out there, how freeing it would be for me. Finally, after years of adversaries forcing me to keep my mouth shut, I was freely speaking out. In any event, I was moving forward on publishing.

I started working on the cover design of my book. Since I was the author, I could do what I wanted with the design. I decided to be like 'Oprah' in 'O' magazine and put my face on it. After all they did take my birth name away, I decided that my face was not copyrighted, so why not use it? If something ever happened to me, people would know who the suspects were. Legal guidance recommended that when publishing the memoir, I included the following disclosure:

"My story is based on my memories that may not be perfect and the names of the individuals have changed to protect the innocent."

Exercising my 1st Amendment rights of freedom of speech, and freedom of press, I was cleared to move forward by the legal system. I was complying.

I emailed a thank you to the legal firm thanking them for good, sound advice.

Legally I was complying, and if they wanted to stop me, they were going to be exposing themselves. Of course, I was not going to release it until I finished my job working at the airport in the city. By then I would be finished and I could blow the whistle. Well wouldn't you know it the job at the airport was stalled indefinitely. I won the bid, but they refused to pay it out, so I was basically unemployed. No time to waste now. I better get the book into publication as soon as possible. Building my new career was going to take time. If I couldn't work in the industry I was born into, I needed to find another watering hole as that one had dried up. Always forward never back. Thinking about the city job, I thought it would be a good idea to lay low, keep the lines of communication open, and show them what a perfectionist I was at my craft. Let them get to know me a little, then once the city OK'd the project, they could judge for themselves.

I turned around in my pink faux fur-covered office chair and stared at the Ms.Pac-Man machine. Suddenly, I started wondering if the machine was bugged. Of course, I knew I could be paranoid, but the more I thought about it, the more it just might have happened. There might have been reason the box was locked and there was no key inside of it. GPS trackers carried a two-week battery life. They had plenty of time to install the device before I picked the machine up. I played music for two weeks straight. I just couldn't trust them. It remains disconnected.

A few weeks later, I bought myself a meditation lamp that contained Bluetooth technology and played music. The Bluetooth connection kept picking up my iPhone. When I was in my bedroom, it would act like a speaker and so, I kept turning the device off.

One morning, I got up and started working. I picked up my air pods to make a phone call, but they would not connect. I put them down finish my phone calls without them, and then went back to Bluetooth. I find a new device listed that was not there before. I kept attempting to turn it off but kept picking up this odd Bluetooth connection.

After a couple of Google searches, I suspected that someone was eavesdropping on my phone conversations. This time I completely turned BLUETOOTH OFF. Since Bluetooth technology is only good within thirty feet, it was either the Ms. Pac-Man machine, or it's on something else that she planted in there.

I received a phone call a few days later. Apparently, Gia had contacted one of my suppliers and wanted to open an account. I was questioned by my supplier as to what the current state of my relationship with her was. I told him that I believed it was a trap, that the girl was a snake, and she will bite you. I told him that I understood how it may be tempting to work with her, but he would be sorry if he did. Now there where so many new questions on my mind.

Back in August, I started working on a new bid. I studied the 1077-page packet in detail over an entire weekend. This was a big job, and a huge break for me.

I stayed in all weekend, went over every word and detail with a fine-tooth comb. I submitted my bid package with implemented changes to the specifications and cost saving measures.

The riots during the summer of 2020 struck our community. Peaceful protests turn deadly, and the downtown stores were boarded. We were living under a curfew and were asked to remain in our homes from 8pm until 6am.

My big break, the project I was waiting for had been delayed due to the exceedingly difficult situation in our communities and the nation.

A month went by, and I heard that I was awarded the bid. My arduous work had paid off. God answered my prayers. After ten years of making lateral moves, I moved up the success ladder.

I started imagining my future. I could hear the key's dangling to my new home. Furniture, towels, dishes, the whole set up was on its way. I made it. My mind set had changed from survival mode into a thriving mentality. It finally happened.

I felt Gia had heard about my success. Why after almost four years did, she reappear on the scene. When we did have the opportunity to speak, she passed on the chance to say anything or show any remorse for her actions.

She said what she needed to that day in the email. And I said what I wanted to and then asked for a cease in communication. But that did not deter her at all.

Three weeks went by, and I get a phone call. There were sharks in the water. Gia was looking to start up an account at the same place I had just become a consultant for. Was it an attempt to cash in on my success? The probable reason could only be jealousy. If it was jealousy, God takes care of those sins with Karma.

The Covid19 pandemic choose her outcome for her. Unfortunately, with the shortages in inventory, supplies, and the backlog of orders, there wasn't enough supply to entertain her, and she was turned away. At which point I found myself thinking... If she came to disrupt my workflow, God protected me. The guest list was closed to those who showed up uninvited. The roles had reversed, and reputations started outshining egos.

Time to think about my safety and look to move out of the area. I heard the Poconos was a good place to not only stand but expand. I started looking for rentals near the water. I was done with this and moving on. I deserved peace and quiet but most of all healing.

# Chapter Twenty

As I sit here today, I am approximately ten days away from publishing my memoir. I sat and thought back to December of 2018 when the dust finally settled, and I made my tiny apartment my home. I put an ad in a law bulletin. I was thinking to increase my chances as the billable hours will restart in January. Early bird gets the worm.

The ad read like this.

ATTORNEY NEEDED! Seeking class action legal counsel ASAP. I am within my statute of limitations and looking to obtain an attorney to take over a fraud claim and three legal malpractice suits. I have expert witness's testimony along with all documents needed to proceed. I just need an attorney that "specializes" in class action law. I have full proof of the fraud that resulted in 14 people losing millions. Fortune 100 companies involved pay is contingent based on outcome. Please email me today to discuss further. Thank you!
Stella Rose at shatteredwindows7@gmail.com[1]

Not one response came back. I had to voice my opinion and tell my story to the jury of my peers one last time.

People ask me what the hardest part was. Why would my family get rid of a top producer? I knew I was being paid less, but I did not care. I was happy just working there.

After Covid19 hit, and my suppliers went down, I started looking

---

1. http://gmail.com/

into crypto currency. Why crypto currency? Why not? Any subject can be researched down to the tiniest detail. Due diligence is key whenever you are investing.

My thoughts on crypto currency were that it is millennial money - digital currency. Its comparable to when I had a beeper in high school. I would get a page and then make the phone call. Isn't that what text messaging and video messaging is today? We can message around the world on social media.

Let us get back to crypto. Crypto is an international currency. When an investor invests in cryptocurrency, they are united with the entire planet. We are brainwashed about put our money in the bank. It will be secure there. No,it is not. Not even a safe-deposit box is safe, as it can be subject to seizure like anything else. I learned from 'Shattered Windows' that my money was not secure in the bank. The opposing council was able to freeze my assets with a court order. I learned about business and survival skills from my father, not from going to school.

International investing on the block chain for example is expansion. If the euro is acceptable all over Europe how cool is it that crypto is acceptable all over the planet. Bypass all the drama at the outdated bank.

It is true, investing with crypto vs. park your money at the bank is risky. It is up to you to secure your own cold storage and have a hard copy of your wallet. Now, if you can do that, you are going to be okay but know that it is vulnerable to cyber-attacks. Life is a tradeoff.

Once you get an advantage one way, there will be an offset. More control equals more work for you independently. Personally, I would rather be in control of my own currency vs. the outdated banking system. The minute that we pool our money together and start controlling how we accept payment, we are now a threat to the government. The United States is a like a massive corporation. We vote as a collective. With crypto currency, we are voting with our dollars. Crypto currency allows us to take our power back.

I think of crypto currency as a long-term commitment. I commit to learning about it, investing in it, and working in the system as a consumer with voting dollars. It is what the stock market was back in the baby-boomer days. Maybe,the baby boomers will still put their money in the bank and invest in real estate. They will use those savings and earnings for their retirement.

My future is not invested in tax dollars that go to other countries without my consent. Crypto competes with the banks. They offer pier to pier money transfer 24/7 worldwide 365.

Crypto takes money out of the local economy and places it in an international pool of investors. My faith in the banks since my previous dealings with bankers is that they hide behind protection laws. Keeping your money in Crypto currency is a risk but so is putting your money in the bank. It is a bit more complicated for your crypto account to be seized because it belongs to cyber space. The crypto companies report income back to the IRS or may not, depending on what platform you use, but looks like the bankers are friends with the government where crypto is more controlled by the investor. Right now, it's limited where we can spend our bitcoins or other crypto currency but the more it gains strength the more it will become spendable anywhere.

The stimulus money that was the result of Covid 19, was a way of luring a mouse into a trap using a piece of cheese. Shut down the economy, then offer people an incentive that will be directly deposited into their bank accounts. Now the government knows and monitors where we bank, and they store all our information in a little database.

Crypto currency is more for the long-term investor, as it takes a commitment to see it fully come into fruition. It can be a ten-to-twenty-year timeline. Thirty-five percent of the money that is out in the economy right now was printed to fill in the gaps. Where did that money go? Are people holding onto their cash? Will cash become a thing of the past with the rise in popularity of crypto? The recent housing bubble was caused by the banks offering low mortgage rates. The people who were in forbearance due to the pandemic would now be responsible for the payments coming due. What drove up the prices in the real estate market was the banks wanting the existing buyer to cover the nut for the seller and avoid foreclosures. Plus, we have a nationwide reduction in new building supplies as we continue to suffer labor and material shortages with the nation recovering from unemployment claims. We are struggling as a nation to get back up on our feet. People do not want to return to work at their old wages as the cost of living driven up by inflation is still out of whack.

The system we are in is we register to vote. When we do that, we get called into jury duty. Jury duty is important if the case being litigated in court ever gets to that point but before it is reached there more than likely a settlement will be made. So, if we want the right to a jury trial, we need to register to vote. Now with this last election I and this is my own opinion, is that the USPS wanted a buyout from the Trump administration during Covid 19 and when they didn't get it, they sabotage him with the mail in votes, or the USPS didn't deliver all the Trump votes only the Biden ones. However,and this is only an idea that came across my mind was that they produced Biden votes and only delivered them. I am not saying that this is true, this is a theory that I thought about. I have no factual evidence to produce these claims, it was only a personal thought. They stole the election from Trump using the mail in votes.

Real estate prices escalated. People think the bubble won't burst, sure it will. Can't you see the banks lowering the interest rates to make it attractive to buy a home (A business model they came up with to sell you a mortgage). The housing prices went up because when the pandemic hit most of us became unemployed and could not pay our share of housing costs. So, the people who couldn't pay their mortgage went into forbearance which meant delayed payments and those promises were coming due. So, the bank has the new purchaser pay the price with the new purchase when the home is valued more. The seller can get a fresh start somewhere else, pay off the bank, and the bank makes a new customer. The bank owns your home, not you. What I learned about the foreclosure process was they allowed everyone else to take advantage of my hard work and maintenance on that home by being able to purchase it at a reduced rate, but they wouldn't work with me. They wanted me out of the way as fast as possible, and fresh blood for the victims to be sucked dry with. In my opinion a mortgage, especially buying at the height of the market is financial suicide. All our credit systems and credit score systems are all outdated like using a commodore 64 computer. For those too young to know what that is, how about a phone book, when is the last time you used one, same concept. Now we are all videos and apps. The first five years of a mortgage is mostly interest so the bank was only interested in a new mortgage they didn't care about me living in that house for ten years, they were not making the money on me like they used to.

No need to hide when your part of the collective is thriving. You want to be noticed so there's more of you to connect with. I love that the millennials are producing APPS so we can all stay connected with the 5D consciousness. Change is good. All the energy that ever existed still exists. Energy constantly transforms. Easier to go with the flow, and flow with your flock.

On May 18th An article written by Gabriel Hays posted on Fox news stated that Elon Musk would be voting for the GOP at the next election because...

The Tesla CEO provided some insight into the reasoning for his political switch, claiming that Democrats aren't necessarily controlled by the people but by special interests.

"The issue here is that the Democrat Party is overly controlled by the unions and by the trial lawyers – particularly the class action lawyers," he explained.

## LA TIMES EDITORIAL BOARD BLAMES 'NORMALIZATION' OF 'VIRULENT WHITE SUPREMACY' ON REPUBLICANS[2]

He added, "And generally if you see something that is not in the interest of the people on the Democrat side, it's going to come because of unions – which is just another form of monopoly – and

---

2. https://www.foxnews.com/media/la-times-editorial-board-blames-normalization-virulent-white-supremacy-republicans

the trial lawyers."

He did ding Republicans a tad, however, claiming their side's problems come from "corporate evil and religious zealotry." Musk has claimed to be a "moderate" in the past.

So right now, I am feeling a lot better about myself because now I know for sure I am not the only one who sees it.

The lawyers are running this country. They write the laws, they pass them, and we are left with "Ignorance is no excuse for the law."

Innocent until proven guilty protects the criminals not the innocent.

And this is what I was talking about when I stated earlier about how 8% of the population runs 92% of the money supply. The good ole boy network TGOBN don't like people like Elon Musk at the top. He's a radical, he's a maverick, he's new blood, he understands the assignment. So, what do they do? They do what they do to us, they find a way to tax him to death. HU$H Money.

They lead us to believe that we elect these officials and then we must suffer with inflation and rising costs and charge us interest on money that doesn't even exist. I predict an economic collapse in this county sometime in 2023. The gold standard was always the only safe standard, not the paper currency. Not crypto currency, only Gold and Silver will stand the test of time.

My housing situation was a struggle. I could not make rent payments due to a lack of work because businesses were being shut down. I was offered rent assistance. It was a great help, but at the end of the day where do I go from here? I certainly see the value of working and moving with a purpose. How do I expand? How can I get ahead? How do I expand my world and go from unemployed to gainfully employed?

I started working on promoting my book, getting the word out there and sticking it in front of every reporter, on social media outlets, and news outlets. I felt that if I was throwing enough out there, something will eventually come back.

So, what have I learned from this whole experience? Well, I need to start writing my own Will. But how do I do that? How can I author a book about estate plans and wills and not have one myself? I researched it and I found this piece to be interesting for my crypto fans.

**Cryptocurrency Will Provision (Footnote 1)**

Including cryptocurrency in your will means you need to balance necessary information and security. An estate planning lawyer can help you and may suggest a provision like this:

I leave all my cryptocurrency investments, crypto-coins, tokens, any other form of digital cash, or anything found in or on my cryptocurrency wallets to [insert name of beneficiary].

My cryptocurrency might be stored on digital wallets, paper wallets, online exchanges, or a combination of wallets and exchanges. The following items or devices might contain a cryptocurrency wallet: _________________, _________________, and _________________. These items should not be distributed to any person until such time as the cryptocurrency, digital cash, or any information related to the access of my cryptocurrency is transferred to [beneficiary named above].

I have created a separate writing from this will that explains how to access my cryptocurrency wallets and online cryptocurrency accounts. This document needs to be kept private as it contains the passwords, PINs, and private keys needed to access my cryptocurrency. This document will likely be stored with my other estate planning documents or [insert specified location(s)]

I am updating my will. And since I can't wait for someone to come by and give me the world, I am going out there and doing it myself. I also need to practice what I preach. I am leaving my mark in this world by leading by example.

I am a Sagittarius, and we blow things up. That's what we do. I used to tell my dad that he should have allowed us to work at other companies so we could bring back (report back) what the big dogs do and implement that into our business model. That is how you grow any business. You learn by example. He was afraid we would abandon him; he could never let us go.

All I am saying is that. If my family contacted me today and asked how they could resolve this problem I would say this.

#1) You have a legal claim against this fake a** lawyer who has broken the law. He has stalked you and used his influence to drain all of us. He is a fraud and we all got robbed. He saw an opportunity and he took it.

#2) Get away from these people as fast as you can. Move out of the area if you must. They are like cockroaches; you can never get rid of them because they do not die. All you can do is direct them in another direction by blowing smoke at them, and then if you are infested with them, you put the light on them, and they scatter.

Whistleblowing is shedding light on the situation, so they will scatter when the lights come on. They thrive in the dark.

At the end of the day, that Lawyer illegally hired himself. He will never prove our father Ok'd hiring him, or that he signed the new Will. He was part of a legal mafia, and he robbed dad point-blank. He charged all of you to fund his legal defense. He needs to pay all the legal fees he charged you back to the estate. He never told us who asked my sibling to contact him, did you really think he was going to oust himself? No way. Deny until you die is what the lawyers say.

I am never going to give up my claim that is a class-action lawsuit. My new job is "Whistleblower." I can stake my claim for as long as I wish because Forgery has no statute of limitations.

I finally realized that it was a game of "smoke and mirrors." The Lawyer was the man behind the curtain. Keep the siblings separated, "Divide and Conquer." The attorney was blowing smoke and clouded everyone's judgment about Gia and I.

Gia and I never cared about the money, at least not until it was stolen by an intruder. We never wanted anything that did not belong to us. All we were doing was making a lawyer responsible for his actions because every single step this person took was fraud. He was the bad guy, not us.

This guy does not want to get caught. He will lose his law license and take the whole firm down with him. Part of the "Woke" culture is to WAKE people up to cases like this. People never suspect the lawyer as a thief because like I said in the book, "It's a difficult task to get one lawyer to throw another under the bus." But what do I know? Anyway, I hope this information helps someone today. Law enforcement was a disappointment and gave me a false sense of security. People put their trust in the law. I say trust in God, it's even written on our currency, everyone else has to prove themselves.

Yes, my family disinherited me financially, but we are still blood, and they need to know who the bloodsuckers are.

I made it on my own, and I am very proud to say that I am in good health and have peace of mind. I made a video regarding my last wishes and sent it to the executor of my will and estate plan. I also sent out backup copies to various confidants because I needed to practice what I preach. Video record your last wishes; we should all know by now after reading 'Shattered Windows' that paper can be changed and manipulated.

Foot Note: 1-Leaving Cryptocurrency in a Will | Bitcoin and Estate Planning | Nolo[3] Reference from

By Erin de Cespedes[4], Attorney

---

3. https://www.nolo.com/legal-encyclopedia/leaving-cryptocurrency-in-a-will.html

4. https://www.nolo.com/law-authors/erin-de-cespedes.html

# Chapter Twenty-one

Where justice is denied, where poverty is enforced, where ignorance prevails, and where any one class is made to feel that society is an organized conspiracy to oppress, rob and degrade them, neither persons nor property will be safe.[1]

Frederick Douglass[2]

If you see something, say something. I was racking my brain trying to think of anyone who could speak up and help me. After all, there were so many players in that game with the Will. Who else knew something? Perhaps there was someone, but maybe I would be the last one to know.

How could Koger hold the dam back and if he was how long could he keep that up? I spoke to an attorney who spent about two hours on the phone with me. What are we looking at here? Forgery, fraud, and negligence for starters. Interference with an inheritance is certain with damages, and retribution.

Who is the right person for me to choose? Which lawyer is going to have the energy to take on this dirty lawyer and his law firm? Until this estate is settled out properly, it is going to continue to come back up. What is the right path to choose? They say you can choose your fate but not your destiny. That means no matter what path I may take; I will end up where I'm supposed to be.

---

1. https://www.azquotes.com/quote/81102

2. https://www.azquotes.com/author/4104-Frederick_Douglass

Until this injustice is fixed nothing in my world will be right. Growth happened when I realized nothing about this is emotional or personal anymore. I followed the money trail and it all lead back to Koger. He has been trying to hold back the dam, but that dam is breaking as we speak.

# Chapter Twenty-Two

Everyone expected me to sue my family, but how was that healing? Besides, they had been taken advantage of as well. There were so many ways of looking at it. I decided to give them the money. Hand it over. I blessed it as it went out and asked the universe to bring it back to me twice blessed.

What good does it do anyone to hold on to the past? It is over and done with. Nothing can be done about it. Even if I wanted to, I could never bring the past back, and why would I want to? There were moments of agony that I would never want to relive.

It is like the number 13, lucky for some people, and unlucky for others. Do you look at the glass half full or do you look at the glass half empty?

Life is like the ocean - it gives and then it takes away. It ebbs and flows. You must learn how to roll with life like you are a pair of skates. If you fight it, it only works against you. That is why they say if you can't beat them, join them.

So, I decided to give them the money and I blessed it - I had to. What good was it holding onto something that was not working? I never wanted anything bad to happen to my siblings. People accused me of having Stockholm syndrome, but it was not true. I knew early on that something was going on. My father raised me to stick with the family so that is exactly what I tried to do. But I was not going to buy into what other people were trying to sell me. I kept my mouth closed, but the wheels were turning, like they always do.

I remember my daddy telling me that the pen is mightier than the sword. At the time I did not really know what he meant, but now I do.

All I kept thinking was "A fool and his money are soon parted."

People asked me if I was receiving death threats and I told them I was. More than that, I was receiving kidnapping threats as well. But what good was it playing the victim role? How did that serve anyone? They were bigger than I was, but it was time to rise.

Heiress definition:

heir·ess

/ˈeris/

noun

1. a woman who is legally entitled to the property or rank of another on that person's death.

"an oil heiress"

o a woman inheriting and continuing the legacy of a predecessor.

"she is the heiress of the talent of her mother and grandmother"

Google July 28,2022

I gave it all up, but I was not about to ever give up on myself. It took a long time to get where I am, but I have finally arrived.

# Chapter Twenty-Three

Yoga is the best physical exercise one can do, in my opinion. It connects the mind the body and the spirit all at once. If you are walking on a treadmill, you are more likely to be watching television or listening to audio or have some other type of distraction while you're getting your cardio in. But with Yoga, your mind checks out and escapes to another other land in the mind.

At any time, you can go straight to Savasana and lay down the entire practice if you want to. If you are breathing, you are practicing yoga. While practicing yoga, the mat is your safe space. If you are taking a class and you are looking at someone else the entire time you are not doing yoga correctly. Yoga is all about no ego amigo. It is a journey of self-discovery and connecting all three parts of yourself as one. I started practicing Yoga in 2002 and I have been in love with it every day since. For me it is life. I can meditate and do my breathing exercises. While I stretch, I can be a part of an entire community. I have practiced in many places and the yoga community is always there for me.

I woke up on a Monday morning and I felt something sharp in my shoulder. I thought back to yesterday's practice and I remember we did "Broken wing pose." I chalked it up to a minor strain and went about my day. I sat down at the computer and felt another sharp pain and soreness all around my neck. I sat and laughed at myself thinking I had overdone the Broken Wing. I took some Ibuprofen and pushed on through my day.

By evening, I laid in bed with ice packs all around my neck and down my left arm. I picked up my phone and started scrolling through the Tik Tok app. I love cruising through all the live feeds. There are so many creators and artists on there and it amazes me how people make their money off some of their ideas. Scrolling, I stumbled upon the "Queen of Cups."

She was making custom drink tumblers. The cup was on a holder that spun the cup towards the camera. I was watching her drop colors onto the cup and with the rolling and swirling of it all, I suddenly forgot everything about my day and all the pain shooting down my arm.

I looked at the clock and three hours had gone by just like that. Before I fell asleep, I hit the "FOLLOW" button. I woke up the next day not feeling any better. For as much pain as I was in, I thought I should have some long exotic story about how I injured myself.

Pushing myself too far in a yoga pose seemed dry as a popcorn fart. I wanted to tell people that I fell off a boogie board while I was surfing in Hawaii and how a Samoan from the five-star luxury resort I was staying at swam out to pull me to shore. But nope, it was just me and my ice packs and my ibuprofen.

Next evening, I was back in bed packed on ice when I flipped on Tik Tok. There she was again, the "Queen of Cups." This time I started reading the comment section and many people were saying the same thing, her live feeds were giving people relief from their anxiety.

She sits in her craft room in her pajamas, off the kitchen of her home and for hours each night she hits the "LIVE" button and entertains thousands of people. This went on night after night for me and each night I was counting cups in my sleep. Night after night I turned to the cup lady for relaxation.

Swiping the comments to the right would lift the comment section and filter off, and the colors would radiate at a higher frequency. At some point I felt comfortable enough to comment with the audience - just very general comments such as how I love a certain color. I would attach heart emojis and leave it at that.

I was still feeling sore, and I could only use my right hand to type into the phone, so I kept all my comments to the bare minimum. This lady was hilarious. She and her husband lived in a rural part of Kentucky, and they were also foster parents.

At the time of her filming, she had adopted three children but stated over the years that they had fostered around thirty-seven. Her little boy would occasionally run past the camera and say something funny that would make the entire audience roar with laughter. There was something about hearing a tiny voice that will warm your heart.

One of the reasons she was so appealing to the audience was because she was so simple and uncomplicated. She admitted that she bought her clothes from Walmart, she liked to eat potatoes chips and drink Mountain Dew Zero. She was relatable to the masses. When she would get riled up about something, she would have these funny Southern sayings that would fly out of her mouth like "Mercy Sakes!"

I went to the Walmart pharmacy to pick up my prescription steroids and there they were, staring me directly in the face – CUP LADY PAJAMAS! I started laughing out loud then realized I was not the only person in the store.

I continued thinking about Cup Lady on my way home and what a wonderful example she was setting for women. You can work from home in your pajamas and have fun all while making a nice living for yourself. I thought to myself, finally someone else gets it!

Night after night while lying in bed, I started making friends with people in the audience. I started to feel like I really belonged somewhere for the time being.

I was a bit aggravated that the one thing I loved so much and dedicated five days a week to was put on hold, but what could I do? For the time being, Yoga was off the table.

By now I had purchased a goose neck phone holder and I was resting comfortably with my stylist pen in one hand ice packs surrounding the other.

Night after night I would emoji heart bomb the audience while sharing laughs with others. It was such a great party and I never felt alone. I started emailing the "Queen of Cups" to let her know how she was helping me through a difficult time for me and how much I appreciated her for all that she did for all of us in the audience. Some nights she would have up to 36,500 people in her room. On average, about 7,500 a night.

Her live broadcasts were catching on and appealing to people everywhere. She started rising and kept going, she became "Tik Tok Famous."

A local newspaper published an article about her about how she got started. After the death of her father the previous September, she wanted to do something about her grief, so she started making tumblers. She said that when she started out on her live broadcast, it was just her and a few other ladies who sat around making the cups and talking about life. Then one day a social media influencer found her, and he was intrigued by her and gave her a shout out. Next thing she knew, she was on TV doing interviews about it.

She shared with us that her business was booming, she started doing Keto and she was dropping weight rapidly. I found this to be relatable. I was doing the same thing, trying out different keto snacks hoping I was finding the magic cure to melt off the Covid weight I had put on. I was writing to her almost every day. Occasionally she would respond with short messages and a smiley face with heart emoji. I told her about when I lost my dad and how it affected me deeply and we connected on that frequency.

People would send her gifts and roses on the live chats that she could later cash in for money. People where so taken by her they wanted to do more. We the audience encouraged her to get a PO BOX and then she finally did. I packed her a care package and sent it out the very next day.

A few days went by, and when she went to her PO BOX, she said that they had to give her a cart because she had so many packages. It brought all of us so much joy. Finally, a way for us to give back to her for all that she had done for us.

She decided to open the packages one night after she finished making all her cups and my box was laying on the floor, but she never saw it. I started mentioning it in the live comments – "The blue box on the floor, open the blue box on the floor it is from me."

Again, she did not seem to register my message. Then suddenly everyone in the audience was commenting with me. She looked around and there was my blue box on the floor. She went and picked it up and started laughing aloud and said, "Oh I thought someone sent us coffee!"

It was true, being the frugal person I am, I used a coffee box I had instead of going out and buying one. She opened the box and put my handwritten letter aside and told the audience she would read it later. I packed the box with all different kinds of Keto-friendly snacks, and she pulled them out one by one from the care package. She said she appreciated it because it showed I was supporting her on her weight loss journey.

At the very bottom of the box was my book. My memoir. I sent her a signed copy because she mentioned she was a fast reader and did enjoy reading books. She put my book on "Blast". Right in front of the camera during her live stream, there it was for the entire world to see. I was discovered on Tik Tok.

A lady in the audience said to me, "You were touched by an Angel" and at that very moment I knew she was correct. I cannot begin to describe how it felt. Her saying that, it sent healing shivers up and down my spine would not even compare to the electroactivity that flowed all over me. It felt like a waterfall of blessings poured over me and I did not ever want it to stop.

The next morning, I went to work same as usual. I walked down the hallway and flipped my computer on at six am. I went to check my sales reports like I do every morning and my jaw dropped to the floor. I saw spikes in my sales just over night. She held my book up for her entire audience to see and they bought it immediately.

I immediately checked all the sales reports from all the places I had my book published. Since I am an independent publisher, I can access that any time I want and it was the same all across the board. Peaks in every format; audible up, paperback up, eBooks, up and up and up and up.

Next, I opened my email and wrote to her. I said it must be our daddy's up in heaven conspiring us to unite. For an entire year that my book was out I took my PR very seriously. I sent it to everyone that had a book club. All the big names including Oprah, Ellen, Sara Jessica Parker, Reese Witherspoon, The Today Show Jenna Bush Hagar, Drew Barrymore, Joe Rogan, Elon Musk,and Ronald Richards a high-profile lawyer on Twitter.

Over the course of the year that the book was out, I did one podcast about it.

A friend of mine who read the book insisted that I sit for an interview, and I did it. I had one person write about it in a magazine and put it on the must buy booklist for Christmas gifts, and I did have mostly all positive five-star reviews but nothing, nothing, and I mean nothing compared to what this earth angel did for me overnight. As she was rising to the top, she blessed me.

By now I considered us friends since I was emailing her all the time and she was responding. I sent her a screenshot of my reports and showed her all the progress she made for me over night.

A few days went by and people in the audience were recognizing me as the author of the book and started talking about it to me. Saying how they purchased it, and they started reading it.

The Queen of Cups was watching the comments and without delay picked up the book and again, puts in on "Blast" and tells people that she already read it and that it was amazing and if purchased it, then I would be one step closer to finding justice for my father.

The pain in my neck and down my shoulder was unbearable. People started messaging me on social media and they wanted to become friends with me and tell me that they purchased my book and that they were reading it. I could only message back short messages because I was still in so much pain.

I was getting a lot of good feedback. I wrote to the "Queen" on the anniversary of my father's passing and told her it was now nine years, and I lie in my bed crying that justice had yet to be served. She mentioned me in her "Lives" and people started praying for me. By the end of the weekend, I was so overwhelmed, my eyes where practically swollen shut and I had cried away all my eyelashes. At the same time, I could see that my book sales were off the charts. People where writing to me and telling me how happy they were, I was brave to have come forward and talk about my experience and even one gentleman told me that he was in law school, and he was reading this and telling his whole classroom about it.

Well, the audience wanted to meet me, and she asked me to come on zoom with her so they could get to know me better. I said I apologize in advance for my appearance because I have been crying tears of joy and of sadness at the same time.

The audience did not judge me, in fact they opened their arms wide and fostered me. All I can remember after the shock of all of it wore off, was she said, "You never know when your next lucky break will come to you. All it takes is just that one person to shout out your name, and then next thing you know your off to the races!"

I did not expect the outpouring of support that was given to me, and I enjoyed it as much as I could.

And then, just like that our spiritual contract ended. I hear people saying, "What is a spiritual contract?" I am a spiritual person. A soul contract or a spiritual contract is when you agree to meet up in this current lifetime and agree to specific terms of your connection. Sometimes we meet people for a fleeting moment, and they are gone as quickly as they arrived. Other times we may spend years or decades with that person, it really depends on what we agreed to before we came down here to earth. It felt an angel touched me, she sent me on my way and that was it. I did not hear from her again. She put me on the map and with no regrets and never looked back.

When I was eighteen, I went to a psychic. I remember reading her postings every week in the local paper. She had her own section and would give you the astrology based on your sun sign for the week. Her office was not too far from the house, so I made an appointment to see her.

When I walked into her office, I was surprised to see a middle-aged woman sitting behind an enormous desk. She had a brown leather high-back-office chair, where she sat patiently while keeping her hands folded. I sat down in front of her and all I kept thinking was why does this little person have a desk this size and laughed aloud in my mind. She started talking to me and asking questions, then suddenly, she got up out of her chair and came and put her hands on my shoulders as she stood behind me. She told me, "You are going to be an author. One day you are going to write books that will prove to be healing for many people." Then she gently removed her healing hands and walked back around to finish the reading.

After I walked out of her office, I started researching spirituality and the study of energy. This was metaphysics and it became my new religion. Spirituality.

Some people never believe in life after death, but I believe in life before our birth. Just because we cannot see things with our human eyes does not mean they do not exist. People spend time exploring space all the time and there are other galaxies and black holes and other universes that we cannot see at all, but we know that they exist.

Manifestations are dreams that we work on continuously to bring to light. For an entire year I worked on getting myself out in front of the public eye and in one second, because of one person, my whole life changed. One lady working out of her home in her craft room on social media put me on the map.

The manifestation in finding justice for my father and exposing the truth about a corrupt legal system was now being exposed to the masses. So much so that I started getting haters. People thought that I was a clout chaser, and that I used the "Queen" for her fame, but that couldn't be further from the truth. People started stalking me online and they were relentless. Any time I checked my social media it was filled with all kinds of messages. Yes, I did have messages how people really enjoyed my book. But there where those I called the "Stella Stalkers." They read me up and down and in and out and started Reddit threads about me, hating on me as much as they could. And all I could do was ask myself, what is the lesson for me here?

I randomly pulled my phone out of my pocket and pulled up the first video with my horoscope on YouTube. Like a scene out of the Twilight Zone the lady giving the horoscope said, "You have haters, and they are all over social media. They are trying their best to dig up dirt on you, but they cannot find anything, and they are not happy."

When your light shines so brightly it disrupts other people's demons. You are doing something right if you have haters. I sat down and questioned all of this and everything that was going on in my world. I went from a nobody to a somebody overnight and I was not afraid, but at the same time I was.

I heard a few rumblings of people wanting to kidnap me and of course they wanted me dead, but I thought to myself, wouldn't they have done all this already? I mean the book was out, the truth was being told, and more than likely an international law firm with a half a billion dollars of billable hours a year is on the verge of collapse.

I kept thinking that the lawyer who did all this was going to commit suicide. On one hand the crimes that he committed were now going to be exposed, and that meant large payouts from his law firm that he is a partner in. On the other hand, it meant that the crimes that he was covering up for other people would now bring those people down. Was the law firm going to collapse like a house of cards? I would eventually find out.

As I said previously, I really do not recommend being a

whistleblower. It ended up ruining my life and my father's legacy. Thinking back about all the people who knew what that lawyer did to me, I wonder why they never spoke up and said anything. I do not blame them for not doing that, but I was secretly hoping that someone would.

People asked me if authoring the book was therapeutic and if I was healed from my situation.

My response was "It was therapeutic, but no I have not yet healed from the situation."

How can I heal knowing there is a killer on the loose. I understand he did not shoot me dead, but he defiantly killed off any kind of life I ever intended to have. At one point, I, was being called the "Homeless Heiress" and I had accepted that as my truth.

I figured the FBI was doing their own investigation, but of course, they were never going to say anything to me about it. I have a big mouth now and they knew I would not help them out at all. Never again would I trust them. Never assume the police or anybody for that matter is "Doing their job." Read my book 'Shattered Windows' and tell me who else I could have contacted? All I could do now is scream the truth so loud I could not be ignored.

So many times, I wanted so badly to be able to sell my family's product. I know that my father created the best of the best of the best, and it was embarrassing to sell for other families. I will say that the people that I have worked with over the years were good people, and I did a lot of great projects with them, but it always felt like I was operating at a loss.

# Chapter Twenty-Four

People who know me - who really know me, (like have my cell phone number know me), will all say the same thing, "She has a heart of gold but there's daggers in it."

Do people from my past have regrets? If they could rewrite the past, would they?

If all I ever did was think about my past, I would be so depressed.

Depression is worry over your past and anxiety is worry over your future. I started living in the moment, but I was very aware of everything around me. They say the power is in the present moment.

What exactly would I do if the FBI came knocking on my door? Well for starters I would not ask them in for a cup of coffee, and secondly, I would not say a word. I had many scenarios that have been running through my mind.

Our legal system is not set up to protect the innocent, it is there to protect criminals, which is why they say, "You are innocent until proven guilty

(beyond a reasonable doubt)."

I could feel that there where people working on my case in silence but what card was left for me to play? Again, the only way I could get justice was to get my story into the right hands.

The reality was that I did have a card to play to receive my inheritance back.

Because how can a judge rule on a case when the files are missing? They can rule on a case, but it would not be a fair trial. Remember there where seventy-four files that were missing from the corrupt file at the courthouse!! If the judge who reviewed the appeal did not have all the information, then he was reviewing information that distorted the narrative, and that is why justice has yet to be served. Until it does, I cannot fully heal. That is what they call a Mistrial, because information was missing. Hello!!

Still today, I am walking around knowing that a HUGE injustice has taken place, and no one has come forward on my behalf.

'Shattered Windows' showed how I never had a fair chance, and since I published the truth in the book, that cracked door, is still an open door.

Who is going to be the one who stands up for justice and serves it?

My father's life ended way too soon. If he had the proper care, he would have lived a lot longer than he did, but the lawyer did restrict him going to see a doctor. The doctor would have written down in the medical paperwork that he was suffering the effects of Alzheimer's and Dementia. We did have paperwork that stated he had it within six months of the will signing but the judge who took an early retirement looked the other way. This is ELDER ABUSE!!

At this point I had so many more options to recover my money. For starters, the law firm who was solely responsible for this mess indeed needed to pay me out and pay out all my siblings including restitution and damages.

Until justice is served, I am not going to stop my fight. I still have a lot of fight left in me, even with a broken wing.

I know I have claims against the FBI, the county, and the court system as well as previous lawyers who all provided ill representation and were negligent.

But who was going to be the one to take the bull by the horns? I started thinking back to the MOB attack on me, and it lines up exactly with how I was pinned up against the door jamb. They nearly broke my neck, and after all this time, I am feeling the effects of it now. I saw my MRI and the left side of the disk is crushed. The doctors asked if I was in an accident?

So, I pull out one of my favorite books of all time, 'You Can Heal Your Life' by Louise L. Hay. Inside this gem is a list of affirmations that you can use to assist yourself back into a healthy body. A path to wellness after a period of discord.

I scrolled down to Neck problems: Refusing to see other sides of a question. Stubbornness, inflexibility. Affirmations to cure to be said daily:

"It is with flexibility and ease that I see all sides of an issue. There are endless ways of doing things and seeing things. I am safe."

Again, I am asking myself, "What is the lesson here for me to learn?"

I was being stubborn because I wanted that lawyer to be caught so badly, I was carrying the weight of the world on my shoulders.

I sat back to think about it all and realized that once again, the universe was speaking to me. The final episodes of Ozark came out. The last of the final season. I watched it before, and I recommended it to people. It speaks volumes about how the FBI cooperates with drug dealers and as long as they get their cut of the money, their department stays well-funded. It is a "New York State of Mind"; look down and then look away. People can say that it is fiction-based, but what I can tell you is, in my experience there is always some truth in every bit of fiction. But New York is a large city and it is the city that never sleeps just like my mind never sleeps because this injustice is still going on.

We grow up believing in fairy tales. You can tell yourself a story over and over until you convince yourself that it is true. The word believe has the word lie in it. As children we watch Disney fantasy movies and read superhero comics. We grow up thinking we are a princess and can accomplish feats beyond what is normal - that good prevails over evil. It is a lie. Sometimes it is not what we make it, but it's what we must do.

For some people, I was a saint in my story, and to others, I was the villain. Either way it was my story and I had to live it and all the trauma that came with it, too.

I remember one time when I was collaborating with this guy who was helping me write computer code for my father's company. I eventually computerized the whole company, but I started out with the smallest department. I hired a man who knew how to write code. When I interviewed him, he told me that he was working as a loss-prevention manager. I asked him what the most intriguing fact about his job was. He answered, "That ninety percent of all crimes are inside jobs." That made sense to me. You would have to know the system in order to get around it.

The FBI uses informants. They get your besties on their side, but you will not know it. They figure whoever stirs the pot usually licks the spoon. So,they find someone who maybe, knows just a tiny bit of information and scare the crap out of them until they agree to cooperate. Since most people are weak, they fold. They drink the Kool-Aid. This is how they take you down. They turn your confidants into informants.

The fish would not have gotten caught if he didn't open his mouth, but the majority of these big moves are not small operations. They go after the big money. They want to skim off the top of the biggest organized crimes. They figure if you cannot beat them, might as well join them.

The way I live my life now is quite different than before. Everyone is at arm's length. When people see what you have, they start thinking of ways they can take it from you.

Nobody is allowed in my home. Unless you are paying the bills, we can meet out in public. It is called privacy. The best way to keep what you have is to keep it to yourself.

You cannot give people anything to talk about. If you want something so badly to the point that it controls you, you are out of control. That obsession is now controlling you, vs. you being in control of your own life.

They cannot do their job if they have no information to feed on.

The best thing you can do is throw them off track. Yes, you are going to lose a lot of people in your sphere of influence, but if you want to stay alive, you have to realize they have an entire team working against you.

Therefore, I wear a body camera now. I started wearing a body camera in 2017 and I feel as though it is the only reason why I am still alive, and telling my story.

The turning point for me was when I still owned my home and was standing on my deck looking over at the pond across the road from my home when I saw a bush move. It felt so strange, and I said to myself, "Did that bush just move?" And then, the bush grew legs and walked around the pond and out of sight.

There was actually someone disguised as a bush, hidden amongst nature that was watching me. That really took some planning on their part - quite inventive. Why he got up and moved while I was outside and allowed me to see him, I am not sure unless "nature" really called, and he had to quickly leave.

We all know that our phones have little tracking and listening devices. We talk about something to someone and the next thing we know our phone is sending us ads about it. We have no privacy, none, not if we are connected online.

As I was blocking everyone, I knew on social media that was pissing a lot of people off. I explained that when I post something publicly, and someone presses the "LIKE" button, it registers that we are connected in some way, and that is a link back to me.

There is no privacy on social media. Your so-called "friends" are like the suckers I used to get as a child when I went to the pediatrician. I would get a shot and then I would get a lollipop. The lollipop never changed the fact that I was poked by a needle, but it did give me the sense of being soothed for a brief time.

This is what a social media "friend" is. As your life changes, as you grow and you get back on your feet, you realize not everyone claps when you are winning. When you start shining your light brightly, it disrupts other people's demons.

Not everyone is happy for your success, and they are happy to be your "friend" when you are low. Pay attention to the ones that do not clap when you win.

Everything in life has a price. You may cut the line repeatedly, but there is always a consequence, and you will pay for doing it down the line somewhere else.

As I was fighting a monetary crisis, someone else was fighting cancer. We are both fighting for our lives but in quite different ways.

One thing I was comfortable with was not chasing the family down for money. Deep down inside, I knew that was the wrong path. I recently looked up the corporate paperwork for my family's business and sure enough, Koger was still on it. He was still controlling their every move.

I kept thinking back about my father when he joined WWII when he was only sixteen years old. The news broke about Pearl Harbor, and he begged his grandparents to sign off on the paperwork to allow him to join the navy and fight for our county. He never gave it any thought that he may never make it out alive. He joined the US NAVY with eighteen of his friends and him and another friend where the only two that survived.

Throughout my whole life my father talked about the War and how it impacted him. It really left him traumatized.

He spoke about how he was on two destroyer ships that sank in the Pacific Ocean.

He invented a tool to assist in firing of torpedo's and later in his life he was recognized for it in the form of a letter that was issued from Congress.

The War and his military mindset were one of discipline. He raised us to be soldiers in his army.

I still could not accept that my family was out to get me, and they made me the sacrificial lamb.

To this day I still feel the need to set them free from this lawyer and this corrupt law firm.

I was tired but I was not dead yet. I had to find the strength to keep going. I still had questions and I needed them addressed. Who will ask these questions for me?

There is a lot to be said about the timing of everything. I had time to go within and quiet my mind, to separate myself from all the legal drama. I was able to start to see things from a distinct perspective.

What would Daddy do? He would tell me to stand my ground and fight like crazy and so that is exactly what I decided to do.

# Chapter Twenty-Five

After the social media influencer and the impact of the online of reviews, I saw a Reddit post that said, "Have you read Stella's book?"

I found this to be remarkably interesting since at one point I was trying to get my book on Reddit but the bot's kept kicking me off. God always laughs at us when we make plans because he already made them for us. Manifestations usually play out differently than we envision them in our minds. At the time I thought my book deserved to be discussed on Reddit and when I failed at posting it on there, months later it showed up there all on its own.

One of the comments said, "I did not read it, but I did Google her and it seems like it is as she said, a sad situation."

Googled me? As far as I knew the story about my life, was not on Google unless you followed a link to purchase my book.

I responded by asking, "You found information about me on Google? Will you share the link to that since I am unable to find it myself."

Response "I found a legal case posted online about you."

My reply "You did? Did you read the book?"

Reddit user's answer was, "No, I have not."

I responded, "If you can find anything at all online about me, please DM me because I would like to review that information. You would have to read the book to understand that any information that you think you may have found about me online would be scattered bits and pieces of reality. Even the Judges on my case, all the lawyers and I, myself do not have all the information about my cases, but you would have to read the book to find out those facts. Anything you may find online is a distortive narrative, and that is the reason I wrote the book; to show how people get away with corruption in the legal system. My purpose was to make people accountable. I understand that accountability is not justice, but it is a start. I can assure you this is not a story about a family argument. It is a story about a carefully organized crime and my life as a whistleblower."

Reddit user answered, "I failed at googling."

Now I was angry. "Most people could not have gone through one tenth of what I had to. Before you judge me on the current chapter of my book that you happened to walk in on, read the prerequisite. What they feed you online is what they want you to believe, not necessarily the truth."

Once the book was out people started coming out of the woodwork and because they saw something special, suddenly they were my best friends. People who I had not thought about in years all said the same thing,

"If I knew things where that bad for you, I would have helped you." Well, I am still going through it. You can still help me.

When the book first came out, fifty percent of the time I thought people commenting were informants. More than likely some of them were. I made sure that I confirmed there would not be any lawsuits against the family or the family business every time I spoke out. I did the little legal disclosure insert; "This conversation is for entertainment purposes only."

Some people who realized I was working my way back up top, no longer found me relatable. They liked it better when I was down and out. We were no longer aligned with the same frequency.

Some people had a much different reaction. They found out that I did cooperate with the FBI initially, and later would not talk. I knew the minute the word FBI came up on the phone, all I would hear is dead space. When the phone calls stop, it's because they want nothing to do with you.

Some people are worried about their phones being tapped. All our phones are being tapped by the way. I have had Siri ask me questions out of the blue.

Everything we do is being tracked, one way or another. I have been conditioned to think this way after I studied Akashic records.

They say everything you think and say is recorded in your Akashic records. It is like always having a tiny microphone on you. I think of it as Karma when God our source energy says, "I saw that."

I know that I am a villain in some people's life, an angel in others a giver to some and a taker to others. At the end of the day, I've always said, "It's not always about you."

I went from standing to expanding. Drafting the book made all the difference and pulled me out of despair.

# Chapter Twenty-Six

I accepted my consequences while not excusing the guilty. So, what happened exactly? I told the truth, exposing corruption and the people doing it did not like it. So now what happens to Stella? She takes off!

Sometimes there is no happy ending. I never found my prince charming; nobody came to save me. I was left shattered. Some relationships teach us about endings.

One thing that was obvious, I was in pain. My health and my quality of life had diminished. I felt all my trapped emotions in my neck. The lawyer put me out of work, so I made it my business to go to work for myself telling my story. He was reason for the pain in my neck. I was out of work due to the injury I sustained because of him. I laid in bed for months. I started going to Physical Therapy and meeting with spinal cord injury specialists, surgeons, pain management specialists, the whole nine yards. Here I lay in bed disabled. Remember Koger was the one that ordered that attack on me. Before this guy came into my life I had a job, I was gainfully employed, owned a home on and on. He is directly responsible for the position I am in because he applied excessive force.

Every time I went to an appointment, I was asked the same question "Where you involved in an accident?"

Each time I would respond, "No, I have not been involved in an accident."

They would continue, "There is a lot going on with your neck. The injuries are indicative of an accident."

"I would remember if I was involved in an accident, and I have not been in an accident," I would respond back.

The insurance company cut off my Physical Therapy because they said that my condition was not improving with the sessions. The next step was to set up a consultation for steroid injections into the spine. I had very mixed emotions about this procedure. I understood that they do it routinely, but the risk if they nicked my spinal cord, was a HUGE factor. I contemplated it for a little while and because I was in so much pain I decided to move forward with the procedure. I needed some sort of relief.

I waited two months for the appointment. The insurance only covered the procedure at one hospital and the surgeon only performed the procedure one day out of the month there.

The morning of my procedure, to calm down the inflammation, I woke up early and after a quick cup of coffee, I took a shower and got dressed, then waited for my ride to show.

Luckily, I qualified for the ride share program because I could not drive. A very pleasant young man arrived on time with a large van. The side door slid open, and I stepped inside. I told him how grateful I was he arrived on time. He was about nineteen years old, and we enjoyed a short conversation about pop culture, and we were on our way. I told him that I would see him in three hours and preceded to walk inside.

I went to the information desk. "Who are you here to see?" The receptionist asked me.

I gave her the doctor's name and told her I was there for steroid injections in my neck.

"Where you involved in an accident?" she asked.

"No," I answered.

"But I get asked about that all the time. The only thing that happened to me was I was assaulted and beat up by five men in 2012. I was hospitalized. The pain is in the same area of my neck."

She continued, "Well, they ask because they want to know if someone is responsible for paying the bill. But if you are not claiming it was an accident then the insurance company doesn't have anyone to go after."

After giving her my personal information, I went up to the third floor and sat waiting for my name to be called. I started thinking if I should file a personal injury claim against Koger and his law firm.

About thirty-five minutes later I heard, "Stella."

I turned around and saw a very short, long hair blonde lady waving at me. I followed her back to a room with a hospital bed and she handed me a gown. She asked me if I had anything to eat or drink.

"I had a cup of black coffee a couple of hours ago."

"You won't be able to have your procedure done today." she told me.

"Why? Because I had a cup of coffee? Nobody told me that I could not drink anything prior to the procedure. All they told me was not to have any ibuprofen, or aspirin for three days prior to the procedure."

I showed her my paperwork. Then I looked at the paperwork again and started re-reading it. I pulled the Post-it-Note off the packet of paperwork and right underneath it, there is was, <u>Nothing to eat or drink six hours prior to the procedure.</u>

I looked back at her and said "When the Dr.'s office called me on Friday to confirm the appointment I wrote all the particulars on the sticky note. They failed to inform me there was no eating or drinking. But it is still my fault for not re-reading the paperwork that they gave to me two months ago. I am sorry."

She simply replied, "You will have to call the office and reschedule your appointment."

I had to ask. "Why is it so important that I am not eating or drinking six hours prior? I thought this was an epidural shot so why do I need to refrain from eating or drinking? They normally do that if they are putting you under anesthesia."

She replied, "You ARE going under anesthesia."

"Well, I was not aware of that. Nobody explained to me what the actual procedure was going to entail but now that I do understand, I will reschedule. Still, it would have been nice if when the office called to confirm my appointment, they reminded me of that very important piece of information. Now I am set back after months of waiting. Whenever I had a dog that needed surgery, they always called me the night before and reminded me of no food or water after midnight. It would have been a courtesy for them to remind me, but that's okay," I said. I turned around and walked out and returned to the waiting room.

Walking past the receptionist she called out, "What happened? You are back already?"

I walked over to her and showed her the sticky note over the one sentence and explained what happened.

She responded to me, "It happens more often than you would think."

I walked over to an area with couches and tables. I started a chain of texts to see if Ride Share could come and pick me up sooner than scheduled, followed by a chain of texts to close friends who were waiting for me to let them know how everything went.

At first, I scolded myself mentally by telling myself that I was lazy for not rereading the information packet, but I decided not to beat myself up over it. I am better than I was, but I am not where I am going. I heard Dory's voice in my head, "Keep swimming. Keep swimming. Keep swimming."

I went home feeling defeated. I thought to myself that there was a reason for everything even if I did not know what it was at the time. I had to place my trust in the universe and move forward.

I knew that I ultimately was being protected by the universe from something. What if the doctor slipped and I ended up paralyzed?

For three weeks I worked in agony and pushed myself to continue. I continued my PT exercises. After implementing everything I was told to about modifying my lifestyle, slowly but surely, I started feeling improvement. Taking everything at a careful and slower pace. All the slight changes started adding up to big relief. I continued to work on my spiritual healing and telling myself that I was evicting this pain out of my body. Not allowing it to live rent free inside of me.

About this time my Yorkie Cupid's health started taking a turn for the worse.

I sat back and wondered about my living arrangements. I was broke again and both Cupid and I were both sick.

I parked my Monte Carlo up on the corner with a for sale sign and because I knew the owner and he gave me permission to park it there, I walked inside to say hi to him. There was a man standing there selling CBD products.

I talked to him about my injury, and he told me his own mother had so much chronic pain that it would take her an hour to get out of bed in the morning.

I told him that I took so much ibuprofen that my kidneys are about to fail any day now. He showed me the product that his mother took and explained to me how to dose myself with it.

I started taking it and after 10 days, there was major improvement with my pain. The numbness on the left side of my body was still evident but the inflammation had diminished. I functioned so much better using this product.

A few days later I checked my mail and found there was a pile. I threw it all on my desk and said, "Tomorrow is another day."

The next morning came, and I sat down with my regular cup of coffee, two Stevia's and whipped cream.

I opened a letter from the insurance company. They wanted me to tell them if I was involved in an accident and if I was, who was responsible for it. Again, I was being asked the same question. What was the universe telling me because now even the insurance company was asking me in writing. I could no longer ignore the signs because they were now showing up in different entities.

I received confirmation from the universe. The universe recognized and was telling me that my neck pain was in fact due to the injury I sustained when I was assaulted at my father's house in 2012. I remembered my conversation with the women who scheduled transportation when I called to schedule my procedure. She told me that she was involved in a car accident, and it took eight years for the injury to fully emerge. My neck pain was absolutely tied to the MOB attack. They nearly broke my neck.

I thought about responding back to the insurance company and enclosing a copy of my bookmark for 'Shattered Windows' but then I regressed.

I could have given the insurance company the lawyer's name who ordered the attack, but how could I speak about that unless I had retained council.

**Part of my healing was letting go of trying to find lawyers to assist me with my claims. I was done with throwing away good energy. That lawyer, the one who did all of this; his was blood money and it took all this time for me to realize that. After I realized it, I decided to never try to go after it again.**

The insurance company was never going to get this guy to pay up and I was unwilling to participate in another legal battle. I rested my case after I wrote my memoir and decided to move on. It was a much healthier choice for me in the long run.

Any money that is mine will find me and it will be with ease and grace.

I decided to throw the letter away. It only had two boxes to check. One that said I was involved in an accident and to provide that information, or the second option, I was not involved in an accident.

I am no longer willing to represent myself Pro Se, and the claim was over two years old. As far as the accident goes, the chances of the insurance company making that attorney accountable was slim to none. Nobody was going to help me so why should I put forth any effort? I said I was done, and I meant it.

Tired of the lessons ready for the blessings.

The best thing that happened to me was authoring the book 'Shattered Windows'. People wanted to see justice served and that meant more of the collective helping me seek out the unjust, and to balance it with justice. I was doing what I could about it.

The lawyer who was, and still is responsible never got caught. Koger very clearly walked away the big-ticket winner. He is a fake, a phony, and a fraud. This person saw my family as a honey hole, and his only motive was financial gain. He figured get them invested with him so he could brainwash them – suck them in. Get them hooked. Get the whole family involved and become financially dependent on him. He involved himself in any way he could so they could not get away and that is HU$H Money. My family is undoubtedly haunted by the things this lawyer did. I am the only one brave enough to speak out about it and expose this. Until Koger meets his maker, if this is my only way to get justice, I am okay with that for now.

It is my belief that they do keep tabs on me. One of the best decisions I made was to relocate out of state. It put me in a new, and fair playing field, vs. corruption in their own backyard. If they were ever going to take issue with this and try to prosecute me, people would know who they were because they know my story.

I was going to use every tool in my arsenal to expose them. They took the best years of my life. I wasted the best years of my life chasing down a fraud and have nothing to show for it, and on top of all that, my neck has changed my way of life and caused me to become disabled. I spent so much time chasing the bad guys it turned me into a cripple. So yes,they won. They got exactly what they wanted, for me to suffer and have no life at all.

If you are blaming my siblings, you're missing the boat. Did you walk down that path that Koger paved for you? Or where you part of the collective that saw through all the fraud? Thank you for being on my on my Journey to Justice. Koger was able to convince a ridiculously small amount of people of his lies.

Turning my pain into power, today I am no longer waiting for justice to be served, because my loyal fans, it is being served every day. Do you think I am hiding anymore? Do you think I should? Why? I was never the person who had anything to hide.

Now the attention is 100% focused on Koger. He cannot escape his Karma. He had friends in high places. He would need to, that is his wheelhouse.

That is how I think they came to poach my father. They came in through the real estate tax bills. They saw the same name over and over and when it became a long list; his name went on their next hit list. It all started with extortion and moved with HU$H Money.

Someday, they will fall like a house of cards because Stella refused to let up on the iron fist. This is the only way it can end. If it does not end badly it doesn't end.

Compared to the way it was, my life is a bed of roses, but those roses have thorns.

As always:

I will see you when I see you!

Love:

Stella

The End for Now

**BOOKS BY THIS AUTHOR**

**Shattered Windows: A Memoir**

I was robbed of $125 million, and I can prove it. This is a true story about how I went from being an heiress to becoming homeless. My father built an empire, starting in his two-car garage in 1953. My parents were married for thirty years, but their marriage ended in divorce. After the divorce, my four siblings and I helped our father's business grow tremendously. We were consistently rated at the top for quality and prompt delivery. We had everything going for us; we were respected in the industry and prospered as a family.

Over the years, my father amassed a significant fortune. Unfortunately, when his health began to fail due to Alzheimer's, an unscrupulous attorney colluded with my three older siblings to produce a doctored estate plan and illegally recorded real estate deeds. This attorney falsified company stock certificates and stole millions of dollars in cash assets. On May 10, 2011, the FBI apprehended my three older siblings. My younger sister and I had no idea what was happening and found ourselves completely cut off from the family and the business, with no communication. Three months later, I stood before a federal judge with no legal representation and no money, as my family had filed multiple lawsuits against me. This marked the beginning of my nightmare.

After enduring seventeen lawsuits over eight years, I decided to write this memoir. Following my father's death in 2013, my sister and I discovered that our inheritance share of $125 million was gone. I was ordered to live under an alias and never publicly reference my family or last name again.

In working with the FBI, I was told, "If you know what's good for you, keep your mouth shut." After eight years, all the puzzle pieces fell into place. I uncovered a blatant, organized scheme to strip me of my inheritance and tarnish my reputation. I invite you to join me on my journey as I strive to expose a corrupt system and reveal the unethical actions of a law firm that caused my family's downfall and my transformation from heiress to homeless.

**HU$H MONEY: The Sequel**

My life is a bed of roses and every now and then I run into a prick. My family fell into bad company, and I was collateral damage.

Continue following Stella on her journey about how being a Legal Mafia Whistleblower impacted her life.

The Trilogy:

The third book in this series is currently in progress.

**Spiritual Gangster**

War of Angels a Documentary on the Death of Aaron Carter Part I of II

The Aftermath a Documentary on the Death of Aaron Carter "Oh No!" Aaron Part II of II a series of ten books.
Book One: I Want Candy Aaron Carter X Jesus Christ
Book Two: Blame it on me Aaron Carter X LASD & ME
Book Three: Fools Gold Aaron Carter X Imposters
Book Four: Do You Remember Aaron Carter X Michael Jackson
Book Five: So Much To Say Aaron Carter X Robert Durst
Book Six: Blockbuster Aaron Carter X Rocky Luciano
Book Seven: Demons Aaron Carter X BSB Gangstalkers
Book Eight: Reload the Wesson Aaron Carter X The Hollywood Reporter
Book Nine: Don't Say Goodbye Aaron Carter X Aaron's Angels
Book Ten: Oh Wee Monique Figueroa X Aaron Carter

## ABOUT THE AUTHOR

Stella Rose AllDay

Stella Rose is an established author who experienced corruption in the legal system. She is a legal mafia whistleblower and a badass.

Social Media Handle: #stellaroseallday

http://www.youtube.com/@StellaRoseAllDay

Get in touch: shatteredwindows7@gmail.com

Stellaroseallday is a true crime author. Legal Mafia Whistleblower
"No matter how hard you try you will never be as good as me"
#Stellaroseallday ©
Her three-part series: The Chronicles of Stella Rose is a trilogy.
Stellaroseallday has authored the 'Shattered Windows' memoir.
Details her involvement in true crime 2002-2020 as a Legal Mafia
Whistleblower
'HU$H Money' is the sequel Life of a Whistleblower
documentary.
'Spiritual Gangster' is the trilogy. (in progress)
'War of Angels a Documentary on the Death of Aaron Carter' Part
I - 2023
'The Aftermath a Documentary on the Death of Aaron Carter' Part
II - 2024
Documenting the death of Aaron Carter multi-platinum
award-winning singer, broadway, television, film, songwriter,
music producer, model, and child star. 'Murder for Hire'

conspiracy theory murder plot. Brother of Back Street Boys singer Nick Carter.

# Epilogue

Moving to Pleasantville was the opportunity to heal myself. I needed this more than anything. I needed this time to work on me. My health took a major turn for the worst, and I knew it was now or never.

This time I turned to the water element, fresh water. Water is essential for life, so I was ready to take the plunge and jump in both feet.

Living in a lake town you adapt to "lake life." Lake life is a year-round resort lifestyle. I am currently a local. The first thing you learn is your friends are going to visit you there more than at your original hometown address. Everyone wants to live this life and it is where I found clarity. It is a perfect location for me at the present time.

The universe allowed me a pleasant place to live, and to realize life really can be pleasant. I have been acknowledged, as a local author and was invited to do a "Meet and Greet" book signing event hosted by the local library. The community opened their arms to me.

Soulmates will meet you all along your journey. You do not have to go looking for them either, just recognize when they show up.

Like I always say, "When you put someone in charge of your destiny, you have already lost control. You and only you determine your success."

**My Dad used to say "Your attitude determines your success."**

**Afterward**

I was not an author, but I have a story. I taught myself the rules of the road. People encouraged me to chronologize the stories surrounding my life and the exploitation of corruption. I had doubts that one lady could change the world, and then I thought about that song by Rachel Platten, 'Fight Song' and I would be inspired every time I listened to it.

"I might only have one match, but I can make an explosion." And that was my inspiration to go on.

I took my life back. I realized I was a part of something so much bigger than being a speck of energy in this world and I utilized every resource that I had. I did not need to put anyone in jail. Koger put himself in spiritual jail. Mentally he imprisoned himself, so this time I was able to free myself like the two of swords in the tarot. I was not being held prisoner, only the stories in my mind were telling me that. Authoring my story set me free and I encourage anyone who feels inspired to write down their story and live your dreams, just like your girl Stella. Love to all and harm to none.